Boston Red Sox players in 1946. Dave Ferriss, Rudy York, Bobby Doerr, Hal Wagner, John Pesky, Ted Williams, Mickey Harris, and Dominic DiMaggio (*l* to *r*) © Bettmann / Corbis.

TEAMMATES

OTHER BOOKS BY DAVID HALBERSTAM

The Noblest Roman

The Making of a Quagmire

One Very Hot Day

The Unfinished Odyssey of Robert Kennedy

Ho

The Best and the Brightest

The Powers That Be

The Reckoning

The Breaks of the Game

The Amateurs

Summer of '49

The Next Century

The Fifties

October 1964

The Children

Playing for Keeps

War in a Time of Peace

Firehouse

TEAMMATES

DAVID HALBERSTAM

HYPERION

NEW YORK

ISBN: 1-4013-0057-X

Hyperion books are available at special quantity discounts to use as premiums or for special programs, including corporate training. For details contact Michael Rentas, Manager, Inventory and
Premium Sales, Hyperion, 77 West 66th Street, 11th floor, New York, New York 10023, or call
212-456-0133.

ORIGINAL DESIGN BY JUDITH STAGNITTO ABBATE / ABBATE DESIGN

FIRST PAPERBACK EDITION
PAPERBACK ISBN: 0-7868-8867-9

10 9 8 7 6 5 4 3 2 1

FOR MY OWN BELOVED TEAMMATE,

NEIL SHEEHAN

TED WILLIAMS

ONE

Ted was dying, and the idea for the final trip, driving down to Florida to see him one last time, was Dominic's. It was in early October 2001, and Dominic was not eager to get aboard a plane and fly to Florida so soon after the September 11 terrorist attack, and his wife, Emily, most decidedly did not like the idea of him driving there all by himself. "I just don't want you driving to Florida alone," she told him. "It's much too far." They had been having dinner at a restaurant in Marion, Massachusetts, with their friend Dick Flavin, a local television personality and humorist. Flavin's boyhood hero, a mere 55 years earlier, had been this same Dominic DiMaggio, then the centerfielder for the Red Sox. Half to herself Emily had added, "Can you imagine? An eighty-four-year-old man driving all the way to Florida by himself." It was said in a way that precluded any argument. "How about this?" Flavin suggested to Dom. "I'll go with you and share the driving." Dominic jumped at the offer and immediately signed on. That gained Emily DiMaggio's approval, something not lightly done. "I know what else, I'll call John," Dominic added, "and see if he'll come with us." John was Johnny Pesky, his and Ted's teammate for all those years, for whom trips to Florida were significantly harder to make.

Pesky loved the idea and he too quickly signed on, and in the way that these things are decided without being formally decided, it was agreed that Dominic and Dick would share the driving and John, 82, would sit in the backseat. As a kind of penance, Pesky agreed not to smoke his requisite two cigars a day. Bobby Doerr, the fourth teammate who had remained so close with the others, would not be able to make the trip. He lived in Junction City, Oregon, and though he made occasional trips back East, usually to the annual Hall of Fame induction ceremony in Cooperstown, New York, his ability to travel had been severely limited after Monica, his wife of 63 years, had suffered two strokes in 1999.

They had, the four of them—Ted Williams, Dom DiMaggio, Bobby Doerr, and Johnny Pesky—played together on the Red Sox teams of the 1940s; Williams and Doerr went back even further: They were teenagers together on the San Diego

Padres, a minor league team in the mid-'30s, and played with Boston in the late '30s. All four were men of a certain generation, born right at the end of World War One within 31 months of each other—DiMaggio in 1917, Doerr and Williams in 1918, and Pesky in 1919. Doerr's middle name, in fact, was Pershing, after John "Black Jack" Pershing, the American general who had led the American troops in Europe in the Great War. On occasion, Doerr had been called Pershing by his teammates in the old days.

They were all four from the West Coast, and three of them, Doerr, DiMaggio, and Williams, started out in the Pacific Coast League, then a top minor league. The other three had encountered Pesky first not as a peer, an up-and-coming young shortstop with uncommon bat control who could hit to all fields, but instead as the boyish clubhouse attendant who worked in the locker room for the Portland Beavers in the PCL. It had been Johnny's job to wash the athletic clothing and shine the shoes of the visiting players, and the players tipped him 25 or 50 cents a game for the service. When Pesky was about to join the big club in Boston in 1942, after leading the American Association in hits in Louisville, the other three, all big leaguers by then, had joked about him: Yes, it was the same Johnny Pesky, you know the little guy who shined our shoes and washed our jocks back in Portland. Needle Nose, they eventually nicknamed him, because of his prominent nose. No one had liked using the name more than Ted, who seemed to think it made Pesky into the younger brother he had always wanted (instead of the younger brother he actually did have, Danny Williams, who was constantly in trouble with the law and thus a reminder to Ted of the fragility of his own hard-won position in life). Pesky's nose was indeed rather long and sharp, especially in relation to his body, which was rather small. The nickname might not have lasted a lifetime, had it not been for Ted, who used it so much that on occasion, when John called the others, he would identify himself simply by saying, "This is Needle."

They were all special men—smart, purposeful, hardworking—and they had seized on baseball as their one chance to get ahead in America. They had done exceptionally well in their chosen field. Williams and Doerr were in the Hall of Fame. Many of the players from that era were puzzled that DiMaggio and Pesky had not been eventually inducted by the old-timer's committee, which took a belated second look at who had made the Hall and who had not. That was particularly true in the case of Dominic DiMaggio, who had been an All Star seven times; Williams himself believed that it was a travesty that Dominic was not in the Hall. None of the four, most assuredly, had gotten rich off the game, not in the era they played in and not in the material sense, for the richness they had taken from the game was more subtle and complicated. A couple years ago Pesky and DiMaggio were together at the funeral of Elizabeth "Lib" Dooley, a beloved Red Sox rooter who was considered the team's foremost fan, having attended every home game from 1944 to 1999, and John had casually asked Dominic how much he had made in his best years. Forty thousand, Dominic answered, and then he asked John the same question. Twenty-two five, Pesky said.

They had after all grown up in a much poorer America when career expectations were considerably lower, when the people who went off to college were generally the people whose parents had gone off to college before them. Two of the four, DiMaggio and Pesky, were the children of immigrants. In DiMaggio's home, Italian was still spoken, and Pesky's real family name was Paveskovich, as his Croatian parents were still known, at least to themselves if not to the larger world. Williams had grown up in what was ostensibly a traditional Scotch-Irish home—what name could be more American than Williams?—but in fact his mother, unbeknownst to most of Ted's friends, was half Mexican.

That was the America that existed before the coming of the G.I. Bill and the postwar meritocracy, which made it possible, seemingly overnight, for all kinds of bright, young Americans, who would never before have had the opportunity, to go to college. Dominic DiMaggio, it was true, had an offer of a college education—he had always done well academically—but he went to work instead. In the case of the other three, the one great chance to get ahead had come through baseball. Looking back through the lens of today's infinitely more affluent America, it seems hard to believe that their choices were so limited. Today it might have been quite different for them: Ted Williams, with his passion for excellence, his outrageous, almost belligerent intelligence, and the sheer force of his unyielding personality, might have become a brilliant brain surgeon; Dom DiMaggio might have ended up as the CEO of a major corporation; Bobby Doerr might have gone to a small college—he is a quiet man, and a big university would have been an uncomfortable experience for him—and stayed on to become, almost to his surprise, the dean, popular with both students and faculty; and Pesky might have become the baseball coach at a large university, where his teams always won, and where in time he was regarded as a legend.

They could all remember the exact moment when they first met each other. In the case of Doerr and DiMaggio, it was in the summer of 1934, when Bobby had just signed on with the Hollywood Stars, one of the two Pacific Coast League teams playing out of Los Angeles. On Doerr's team that summer was Vince DiMaggio, the oldest of the three DiMaggio brothers who played pro ball. (Of them it was said that Joe was the best hitter, Dom had the best arm, and Vince, who wanted to be an opera singer, had the best voice.) As a young man, Vince was the most outgoing of the brothers, and when the Hollywood Stars played in San Francisco, where his family lived, he often brought his teammates home for a meal after the game. "It was great fun going there," Doerr remembered. "The food was wonderful, and Mama DiMaggio was so generous—there was always a lot to eat. I loved watching the veteran ballplayers try to drink Papa DiMaggio under the table. He made his own wine in the cellar as people did in those days, and these old-line ballplayers would come in, and they would drink the wine hard and fast the way they drank whiskey. Mr. DiMaggio—he always had this little cigar in one hand—would just hold his glass and sip it slowly and watch them, and pretty soon they would go under the table instead."

One day that summer Vince took several of his teammates fishing in the Bay, out near Alcatraz. Afterwards they had docked in the harbor, near the place where the family restaurant would one day stand, and then they all walked over to the DiMaggio house. "There were about four or five of us going over to Vince's house for dinner," Doerr recalled, "and there was this little kid coming down the hill, quite small, I thought, and quite young looking, though actually he was a year older than I was. Vince spoke to him and someone asked Vince who that was, and he said, 'That's my brother Dom.'"

"I remember the meeting very well," says Dominic, "because they were all professional ballplayers. There was Bobby, and Archie Campbell, and Frank Shellenback, who was the Stars' manager, among others, and I thought Bobby looked very young to be a ballplayer. I thought to myself, He's just a kid. He might be younger than I am, which he was by a little more than a year, and he's already playing pro ball. But I also remember that he was nice. Bobby was always nice, and he was not stuck up. It hadn't gone to his head that he was a pro ballplayer, not like it would have with a lot of guys. Nothing ever went to Bobby's head."

What the other three remembered about seeing Ted Williams for the first time was that he was so tall and skinny, and looked so goofy. The idea of him as a pro ballplayer, let alone the great pro ballplayer and the great power hitter he would one day become, seemed most unlikely. No one that skinny could be a ballplayer, they all thought. "Six foot three and one hundred forty-seven pounds, the skinniest thing I ever saw," Doerr remembered. Dominic recalled his first glimpse much the same way: "Like a broom holding a bat."

Doerr remembered his first glimpse of Ted. It was June 1936, and the original Hollywood Stars had just moved to San Diego and been reborn as the Padres, after Bill Lane, the owner, balked at a 100 percent rent increase for Wrigley Field, the ballpark the Stars and the Los Angeles Angels shared. Some San Diego businessmen induced Lane to move the team south to what then was a city of only 200,000 people. It was right before a game, just as the regulars were taking batting practice, when Williams, who had been playing for a local school, Herbert Hoover High, was brought in for a tryout. "I was standing right near the batting cage," Doerr remembered, "on the first-base side—I don't know why I was there, but I remember the scene distinctly. And here is this kid, and he is really skinny. You wanted to laugh—no one that thin could possibly hit. 'Let the kid hit,' Shellenback is saying, because he's been told that by the owner, Bill Lane, who wants to look at Ted. The veterans are all grumbling—you know, we all wanted our batting practice swings. No one thinks he can be a ballplayer, he's much too thin, and we've got a game in an hour or two, and he's not even going to play with us. So we're impatient and there's a lot of resentment, a lot of muttering. And then he started to swing. And we all remembered that swing. You paid attention to the swing. He hit six or seven balls very hard, and all the veterans are starting to watch, and it's getting very quiet, and I remember one veteran player saying, 'That kid is going to be signed before the week is out.' "

Dominic DiMaggio remembered a similar scene. "It was my first year in the league. It was early in the season. I was playing for the San Francisco Seals, and we were playing San Diego. I wasn't starting yet. Brooks Holder was our centerfielder, very fast, but he couldn't catch the ball, so there was going to be a place for me. Lefty O'Doul was our manager. The other guys, the San Diego players, are taking batting practice, and eventually Ted comes up to take his swings. And suddenly Lefty, who was a great hitter, and a great hitting instructor, jumps up from our dugout and goes to the other side of the field, near their dugout. That's very unusual—you just didn't do that in those days. And he waits there, and finally Ted finishes his swings, and Lefty calls him over, and they talk for a little bit. Maybe twenty or thirty seconds. And then Lefty comes back to our dugout. And we're all sitting around, and someone asks him, 'Skip, what was that all about?' And Lefty says, 'That kid is one hell of a hitter. And all I told him was, "Don't let anyone ever tamper with your batting stroke. Just don't let anyone ever touch you." ' "

Johnny Pesky didn't connect with Williams until later. He had seen Ted in the locker room in Portland often enough, but had never really talked to him. In 1941 Pesky played for

Louisville, Boston's top farm team, where he hit .325, led the league with 195 hits, and was named the league's MVP. The next spring Pesky went to spring training with the big club in Sarasota, Florida. A few days after he arrived he went to dinner with Bobby Doerr, whom he had known from his Portland days, and who was probably going to be his double-play partner. Ted had not yet arrived because he was having some trouble with his draft board, but in the middle of the dinner he showed up.

"You're the kid from Portland, right?" Williams asked Pesky.

"That's right," Pesky said. He did not say "sir," although he felt like he ought to because this was the great Ted Williams, the man who had hit .406 the previous season.

"They tell me you're a pretty good hitter," Williams said.

"That's right," Pesky repeated, not quite sure what his role should be in this conversation, but he was not about to give ground, either—little guys should never give ground to big guys, even in conversation.

"Well, if you can hit .280 you can help us," Williams said.

"Hell, I can do that just running out infield hits," Pesky answered, not lacking in confidence. ("I think at the time Ted thought I was kidding, and then when he saw what kind of hits I got—so many of them in the infield, so many of them really cheap—he knew I had been telling the truth," Pesky said years later. In fact he liked to tell of his first time in Yankee Stadium—he had been hitting quite well early in the season and he stepped in to take his pre-game batting practice swings, and a number of Yankee players, as well as some of his own teammates, were gathered around the cage to take a look at this new Boston star at work. Properly nervous with Joe DiMaggio, Charlie Keller, and Tommy Henrich all watching, Pesky proceeded to hit a series of cheap, little grounders. "How can this guy be getting all those hits?" Keller asked. "Why, he can't get the ball out of the infield." "Hey," Williams had answered, always ready to stick it to Pesky, "those *are* his hits.")

For their entire careers they were basically one-city, one-organization men. Only Pesky played for any team other than Boston, when, at the tail end of his career, he was briefly with Detroit and then Washington, but the others felt those years and those at bats did not really count. "We were all lucky to play professional ball, and, even more important, to play in Boston, which was such a great baseball town and a good organization. We were like kids in the candy store," Pesky recalled. "We felt very lucky to be in Boston," Doerr agreed. "I was always afraid of being traded. Once in the late 1940s there was some talk in the newspapers about trading me to Detroit. We had a kid named Chuck Koney, who was playing second base in Louisville and doing well, and we were always short on pitching, especially after Dave Ferriss and Tex Hughson came up with bad arms. So, the talk was that I would be traded for one of the Detroit pitchers—they had a lot of them. It was probably going to be Dizzy Trout. And I was really scared. Detroit was a good baseball town, but I loved Boston: the fans, the ballpark. I didn't want to leave, and fortunately the trade never came off."

That was something unusual in baseball: four men who played for one team, who became good friends, and who remained friends for the rest of their lives. Their lives were forever linked through a thousand box scores, through long hours of traveling on trains together, through shared moments of triumph, and even more in the case of the Red Sox, through shared moments of disappointment. They were aware that they had been unusually lucky not just in the successful quality of their careers, but also in the richness of the friendships they had made. And they were all too aware that it was unlikely to happen again, that the vast changes in the sport, especially free agency, made rosters more volatile while the huge salaries somehow served to lessen the connection among teammates rather than solidify it. They and others who followed the sport realized there was less continuity and community on teams. Of one Red Sox team of the '70s it had been said that when the team plane landed, the players quickly dispersed on their own—"25 players, 25 cabs."

It was different for the four of them, coming as they did from so different an era. After they stopped playing, they kept in touch, continuing to pay close attention to each others' lives. When Dominic was diagnosed in 1962 with Paget's disease, a rare and cruel disorder that causes enlarged or deformed bones, the others were acutely aware of his ordeal. "Dommy's got this goddamn awful disease, and it makes him bend way over. It's a real mean son of a bitch of a disease, but he's the proudest goddamn human being you ever met. Anyone else with a goddamn disease like that loses dignity. Not Dommy," Williams told me years ago. "Dommy doesn't lose his dignity."

When Pesky, about 20 years ago, began to lose weight at a frightening rate, they were all very nervous. Ted was sure Pesky had cancer. There was no lack of good medical facilities in Boston, but at first the tests revealed nothing. "I'm worried about our needle-nosed little shortstop," Williams told the others. Phone calls—many of them loud, because Ted seemed to shout even in normal times, let alone when he was upset, and he was very upset over the lack of a diagnosis—were made from Islamorada, in the Florida Keys, where Ted lived, to various Boston doctors and hospitals, even though Pesky, a local icon, was already getting the best treatment imaginable. Pesky himself was afraid that he had some form of cancer by this point. His weight, around 170 pounds in his playing days, had dropped alarmingly, and he was below 130 when the doctors finally discovered the cause: He had become allergic to wheat. "Perfect for someone of Croatian origin—that's all we eat," he noted.

They had all been aware as well of the problems with Monica Doerr's health, and of Bobby's abiding, loving care for her. She had developed multiple sclerosis back in the 1940s, and though it stayed for a time in remission, it flared up again in the 1960s. The others were aware of her pain, how much harder her life had become because of it, and, of course, of Bobby's constant tender care of her, his determination that they would go on with their lives as though she was not sick, that they would travel as they had always done, as if her health imposed no limits on their vistas.

Now as the men headed south to Florida, both DiMaggio and Pesky knew this was the last time they would be with Ted. Dominic had been talking to him every day, and Ted seemed to be slipping away right in front of him. There had been a leaky valve in his heart, and there had been very little the doctors were able to do about it, and over time it seemed as if the strength was simply ebbing out of him. He was in a wheelchair in Hernando, Florida, and he had suffered two strokes, and he was, they knew, going fast. They knew as well that one of the reasons they had all stayed friends was because of Ted, that he was the most compelling personality among them, not just the best ballplayer—perhaps the greatest hitter of all time—but the most dominating personality as well, both generous and combative in the same instant, ever tempestuous, the man child who dominated every conversation, who shouted others down, who never lost a single argument to anyone. Joe DiMaggio might have hit in 56 consecutive games, a seemingly unrivaled record, but he never won 33,277 arguments in a row, like Ted Williams, the undisputed champion of contentiousness. Ted Williams *never* lost an argument, in no small part because he was bright and he marshaled his facts and argued well, but also because he shouted all the time and appointed himself judge and jury at the end of each argument to decide who won. He never lost an argument because he was Ted Williams. In his playing days, he would be there every day in the clubhouse, holding forth—the Ted Williams Lecture Series—at least a speech per day, orating and arguing at the same time. Mel Parnell, the great Boston lefty, told me you failed to listen to him at your own risk, because for all the stuff you did not need to hear, there was always so much to learn, often about hitters on the other team, because he was so smart, and he missed nothing that happened on a ball field. "I can," John Pesky said 60 years after he heard the basic lecture for the first time, "still hear him telling us, because he said it again and again, 'You'll get one good pitch to hit. One good pitch. That's all. Don't count on more. So you better know the strike zone. And when you get that one good pitch you better hit it and hit it hard. Remember, just one good pitch.'"

For many years, the glue that held them together as friends was Williams; someone that great, one of the very best ever at what they all did, had rare peer power. "It was," Pesky once said of him, "like there was a star on top of his head, pulling everyone toward him like a beacon, and letting everyone around him know that he was different and that he was special in some marvelous way and that we were that much more special because we had played with him."

He might not, the other three teammates knew, be the easiest man in the world to deal with. He always did what he wanted and never did anything he did not. But to no small degree he was the one who had kept them friends; they stayed close because he willed them to stay close. In a way they had become his family—his real family, the one from his childhood, had been difficult, always causing him more pain than plea-sure—and there was an awareness that Ted was always there for them. (This was true as well for some of Ted's other teammates, who were far less successful financially than Pesky, Doerr, and DiMaggio and who badly needed Ted's help later in life. If a former teammate was living near the poverty line, Ted would somehow find out and quietly make sure that he had enough money.)

In the beginning Ted had been closest to Bobby Doerr. Bobby was five months older, but infinitely more mature, with an uncommon emotional equilibrium that would stay with him throughout his life. He never seemed to get angry or to get down. This stood in sharp contrast to Williams' almost uncon-trollable volatility, and his meteoric mood swings. It was as if Ted had somehow understood the difference, that Bobby was balanced as he was not and that Bobby could handle things that he could not. Ted somehow understood that he needed Bobby's calm, and he seized on his friend's maturity and took comfort in it from the start.

But in later years, as Ted's health began to fail, Ted became closer and closer to Dominic. He had always called him Dommy, as if he too were a brother, and eventually, late in his life, Dom started calling him Teddy, and speaking of him too as someone who was as close as a brother. By that time they both lived in Florida, and Bobby was 2,500 miles away in Oregon, and increasingly preoccupied with taking care of Monica.

In the late 1990s, as Joe DiMaggio's health began to fail, Dominic got deeply involved in trying to take care of his brother. It was at that point that Ted began to call Dominic five or six times a week, wanting to know how Joe was doing. That of itself was fascinating. Joe had played for the Yankees, Boston's bitter rival, and the two great hitters—Joe, who hit in 56 straight games in 1941, and Ted, who hit .406 that same year— had had their own unspoken rivalry. They were at the center of one of the great ongoing debates among baseball fans of several generations, as to who the better ballplayer was, and what might have happened had each played for the other's team, in the other's ballpark. The summary judgment: Joe was the better all-around player; Ted, the better hitter.

The two had not been close when they played. Joe DiMaggio was the most aloof of men; he held out genuine warmth and friendship not even to his younger brother or his long-time teammates, let alone to Ted Williams, the one baseball player against whom he was constantly measured. Ted, by contrast, was far more open, far more generous, and far more volatile. After they quit playing his only real connection to Joe, other than through his admiration for him and his love of Joe's younger brother, was the fact that for some 50 years they stood together atop the same pedestal of excellence, honored and celebrated at countless baseball dinners, posing for a seemingly endless number of photographs reflecting baseball's royalty from an earlier age. The byplay between them on such occasions was, more often than not, quite stilted.

Because they had shared so much of an era, even if they had shared nothing else, their mortality was in some curious way a shared one; if they were linked in life by greatness then they surely would be linked in their obituaries. If Joe, who was nearly four years older than Ted, was dying, then Ted's mortality was at stake as well. The imminent death of Joe DiMaggio meant that an era that belonged to Ted, as much as it did to Joe, was coming to an end. Thus when Joe's health began to fail badly in the fall of 1998, and when it became clear that he was dying, Ted was deeply moved and his regular phone calls to Dominic started, always at the same time of day. As soon as the phone rang, Dominic knew it was Ted calling about Joe, wanting to know how he was, whether he was doing any better, asking what the doctors were saying. When Joe died, Ted took it, his friends realized with surprise, like a death in his extended family.

It was not the first time Ted paid that much attention to Joe. He had from the start loved Joe's swing, pure and powerful at the same time, and when in 1996 a talented young Red Sox player named Nomar Garciaparra was breaking in, Ted quizzed Bobby Doerr on the phone about Garciaparra. Bobby had spent much of his life failing Ted's impromptu quizzes, and this time as the questions came in—"Who does he remind you of? Goddammit Bobby, who does he remind you of? You ought to know that!"—Bobby knew somehow he was going to fail again. "DiMaggio," Ted said, finally supplying the answer to his own question. "That beautiful swing, Bobby, it's like watching DiMaggio again." "Dom?" Doerr asked. "No, Bobby. Joe," Ted answered.

Back in 1941, when Joe was on his record-breaking hitting streak, Ted played left field, and he would talk to Bill Daley, the Fenway Park scoreboard operator, who always had a radio going, picking up all the baseball news from around the country. He would yell, "Hey, Ted, he just singled." And Ted would pass it on to Dominic, who was playing in centerfield.

So it was during those long months when Joe was dying that Dominic and Ted became closer than ever. They had always been friends, bolstered by Williams' enormous admiration for Dominic as a player and even more as a man. The respect was not just about Dominic's abilities, but his intelligence as well. Ted Williams surely had one of the highest IQs among the players of his era, and he judged other players not just by their athletic talent, but by how smart they were about the game. He was acutely aware that Dominic was an uncommonly intelligent player, who used his intelligence to overcome any physical shortcomings. In fact, Dominic's shrewdness and intelligence were legend among all his teammates—even if he was never showy about it. When Babe Martin was trying to make the team as a third-string catcher in 1948, he went to Dominic for advice. Joe McCarthy, the manager then, had just come over after many successful years managing the Yankees, and it was obvious to many of the Boston players that he thought the current crop of ballplayers were soft, especially the current crop of Red Sox. Dominic had thought for a moment and told Martin he knew something that would help. "What?" Martin asked. "Wear your shin guards when you take batting practice," DiMaggio advised. "You'll look like you're working so hard that you didn't have time to take them off. McCarthy will like that." Martin took the suggestion, and he made the team, though he would get only four at bats that year and two the following season.

Williams had always respected Dominic's independence as well, the sense he gave off that he was his own man and that no one could intimidate him. There had been a moment when they were young, when Ted was holding forth after a game, as he usually did, filled with whatever point he was making, obliterating all dissent. Everyone else in the locker room seemed not just to be listening but agreeing. Then Ted looked over at Dominic, who had a little smile on his lips, and suddenly he interrupted his monologue. "Dommy, you think I'm full of shit

don't you?" Ted asked. "Why do you ask that?" Dominic re-
sponded. "Because the look on your face says so," Williams said,
laughing. Williams was so smart, he knew long before the others how strong a man Dominic was, that he had surprising
reserves of inner strength available whenever he needed to
summon them.

As they grew older Ted's admiration for Dominic continued to mount. Part of it was that they both lived in Florida and
thus Dominic was able to help Ted out when he needed it. But
a more important part had to do with measures of success beyond baseball, and Dominic DiMaggio arguably was one of the
most successful players of his generation in his post-baseball life.
After he stopped playing, his career did not depend on his baseball success; he did not become a beer distributor or a sports
store owner or an announcer. Though he never went to college
and was seemingly ill prepared for a life other than one in baseball, he simply walked away from the sport on his own terms,
retiring when his skills were still near their peak, before the
Red Sox had a chance to trade him, and he had thereupon
started his own manufacturing company, which made uphol-
stery and synthetic carpets for cars. The company was uncommonly successful, and over the years Dom became quite
wealthy. In time he turned his business over to his son, Paul, but
he did not retire. Instead he continued to make various deals
and play the stock market.

His own personal journey into the fullest of lives was a remarkable one. He had begun as the son of poor immigrants

with marginal career choices and he had become over the years a man of means, graceful, elegant, and wise. If he had not been as great a ballplayer as his celebrated brother on the Yankees or his celebrated teammate on the Red Sox, he had become a more complete and successful human being than either. As Dick Flavin once noted, "I think both Ted and Joe were aware of it, how well he had dealt with his life, and what a complete life it had been, and Ted to his credit admired him for it, and Joe, I am afraid, resented him for it."

Late in his life, Ted Williams would on occasion compare himself with Dominic and find himself wanting—it was the rare comparison in which Ted Williams ever came up short in his own estimation. He would tell Dominic that he had made something of a mess of his life and that Dominic was the more successful one. On such occasions Dominic would tell him angrily, "Stop this Teddy! Stop this now! I never want to hear you talk like this again! You're Ted Williams! You're an American hero! You served your country in two wars. You're one of the greatest baseball players of all time. Millions of Americans look up to you! You cannot talk this way about yourself! There's not a CEO in this country who's done as much as you to make this a better country! I won't stand for it." That would end it, yet in those brief moments of self-doubt, there was rare insight into the way Ted Williams sometimes thought about himself. But moments like that made for an unusually strong friendship because of each man's immense respect for the other.

In 1990 Dominic published a memoir of the 1941 season,

Real Grass, Real Heroes. It was brought out by Zebra Books, a small New York publishing house, and there was a publication party for the book at Tavern on the Green, a popular restaurant in Central Park. Ted flew up from Florida for the occasion, but Dominic, who was famous for keeping things to himself, told no one from the publishing house—he was not about to cash in on his old friend's fame. So it was something of a surprise to the publishers that one of America's greatest sports icons had shown up, unannounced. Of course, he became the focus of the party, dazzlingly handsome, better looking as he aged, full of energy, ready to talk to any and all about any subject, and, of course, ready to give out batting tips.

Dominic loved it as the party swirled around Ted, amused by the sight, by the fact that the old magic still worked. The publisher had scheduled a dinner afterwards for the author and a few friends at the "21" Club, a fancy Manhattan restaurant, and Ted was invited to join them. Well that was damn nice of them, he answered, but he had an old teammate, Jerry Casale, you know, a damned good guy, and he now had a restaurant of his own in this town—Pino's down on 34th Street. He had told Jerry, who won 13 games as a Red Sox rookie in 1958, that he was going to eat there and so he damn well was going to go there and eat at his old teammate's place.

The publisher thought about that for a moment, and the attractiveness of the "21" Club dimmed a bit, and he suggested that they all go down to Pino's instead. Soon after the entire party packed up and took over Pino's. Pino's, it should be noted, is not exactly a chic restaurant; for reasons that remain inexplicable to me it is not listed in the latest Zagat's survey of restaurants in New York. If it were, I think, it would be described like this: "This old-fashioned and unhip Italian restaurant, more Southern than Northern, has a warm and comfortable ambiance, and has the flavor of a '50s hangout. It serves hearty portions of traditional favorites and is popular with neighborhood regulars and sports stars, both present and past. Anti-smoking fanatics should stay away. The warm and outgoing owner once pitched for the Red Sox, and the walls are covered with mementos of that time." Indeed, back in the simpler age when American League pitchers still batted, Jerry Casale, in one of his few times up in Yankee Stadium, hit a home run off the great right-handed Bullet Bob Turley. Casale's brother, Lou, just happened to have taped the radio call of that unlikely moment, and Casale loved to play the tape for the benefit of new customers. Sure enough in the background din at Dominic's party, there was the voice of Phil Rizzuto, who himself had on occasion helped doom these same Red Sox players, now as an announcer, saying, "A home run! Holy Cow! Did he hit that one!"

That night everyone crowded around a giant table, and enormous platters of food were passed around. Dominic sat savoring the entire scene—Flavin had never seen him quite so happy, basking in the warmth of his family and the friendship with Ted—and repeating, "Teddy, Teddy, it's just like the old days on the trains."

Ted had been right: His own mortality was connected to that of Joe, and it was not long after Joe's death that Ted's own health began to decline at a frightening rate. In the final months of Ted's life he would turn to Dominic and say, "Dommy, you're the only one I have left," which meant, Dominic thought, that of those who had been close to Ted so many had died, and so many, like John or Bobby, lived far away and had problems of their own, so that only he was at hand to help Ted out.

In the summer of 2000, after Ted had an operation to stem the deterioration and was in rehabilitation in San Diego, it was Dominic who went out to see him. That was an unusually painful visit, Dominic recalled. Ted was in terrible shape. On the first day, he never even opened his eyes. The next day he opened his eyes for a time, but he was so weak and disoriented that it was terribly unsettling, and Dominic left the room in tears. Gradually, though, Ted rallied, and after he got home Dominic was able to talk to him on the phone, and when their call was finished, Dominic would call Bob and John to fill them in.

TED WILLIAMS AND JOHN PESKY,
FENWAY PARK, 1943

TWO

John Pesky, Dick Flavin, and Dominic DiMaggio,
October 2001

or Dick Flavin it was the trip of a lifetime. He had grown up in the Boston area, a devoted Red Sox fan and the son of a devoted Red Sox fan. He was both historian and keeper of the flame—when in 1989 I published *Summer of '49*, about the Boston–New York pennant race, won

27

by the Yankees on the last day of the season, he paid me the high compliment of sending me a small part of the old Green Monster, the Fenway left-field wall, as a gift. Flavin was born in 1936, a year before Bobby Doerr came to the Red Sox as the first of the young players who would start the Boston club's renaissance.

Flavin started following the Red Sox during World War Two, while Pesky was serving in the Navy. At first his favorite player was Eddie Lake, a popular, diminutive shortstop signed to fill in for Pesky. In 1943 and 1944, Lake hit just .199 and .206 respectively, but the poverty of those batting averages seemed to have escaped the notice of the young Flavin. He was devastated when the war was over and Pesky returned; Eddie Lake was sent to Detroit, traded for the aging Rudy York (a seven-time All Star who thereupon had his last great season, knocking in 119 runs in that marvelous year of 1946). How, Flavin wondered, could they do that to Eddie Lake, to Flavin's mind the star of the team? Who was this Pesky? Who was Rudy York?

This Pesky had in fact led the American League with 205 hits, coupled with a .331 batting average as a rookie in 1942, and then in 1946 rejoined the Sox without a hitch to hit .335 and lead the league in hits (208) once again. It would soon dawn on Flavin that there was more to baseball than Eddie Lake, that the people in the Red Sox management quite possibly knew what they were doing, and that he had best pay attention. He fell in love with the great pennant-winning 1946 team, and his favorite player became Dominic DiMaggio.

There was a reason for this: As a boy Flavin was small and bespectacled. The latter was a painful condition in those days, when the mere presence of eyeglasses was a sure sign that the wearer was doomed to be smart and unathletic. He would probably grow up to be successful, doing some job that smart people did, rather than one that popular kids ended up doing, like playing professional baseball. Flavin loved baseball, but, alas, he could not hit the ball out of the infield. Inevitably, his nickname was Four Eyes. But, miraculously enough, Dominic DiMaggio was small and wore glasses—the rare baseball player of his era who did—and he was a very good baseball player. A perennial All Star, he was said to be serious, intelligent, and well liked by his teammates. For Flavin, seeing Dominic play was hero worship at first sight.

The relationship, it should be noted, remained one-sided for almost 30 years. But in 1974 Flavin, by then a humorist-feature reporter for a Boston television station and a local celebrity himself, met his hero at a benefit at the New England Aquarium. Both Dominic and Emily DiMaggio were there, and Flavin introduced himself to his hero and told Dominic what he had meant to him in an earlier and less happy time in his life. Dominic turned out to be more than gracious—he knew who Flavin was, watched him regularly on television, and liked the offbeat satirical pieces he did. That the great Dominic DiMaggio admired Dick Flavin professionally seemed to Flavin almost beyond comprehension. It was like having the prettiest (and least attainable) girl in your high-school class announce her undying love for you some 25 years after you both graduated. Had there ever been a sweeter professional moment for Flavin? (In truth, I know something about that kind of experience. I was touring a number of cities to promote my book *Summer of '49*, and in Cleveland, I did a midday television show with Bob Feller. Feller was the greatest pitcher of that era, and when the show was over, he brought my book over and asked me to sign it. There I was, David Halberstam—who also, it should be noted in the interest of total disclosure, wore glasses at an early age, though I had a pretty decent left-handed swing, and I like to think I could drive the ball out of the infield—giving an autograph to Rapid Robert Feller, as the sportswriters used to call him, and who was, as every young baseball fan of my generation knew, from Van Meter, Iowa.)

Dominic DiMaggio lingered at the benefit to talk with Flavin, and Flavin left thrilled by the encounter, deciding that he had chosen his hero wisely. A few weeks later he was dining at a local restaurant when a waiter brought over a drink and said that a gentleman had sent it. Flavin had looked up to discover that the gentleman was Dom DiMaggio. Thus was born an enduring friendship, and since Emily DiMaggio, a civic and community leader of unusual dynamism and passion—the Queen, Ted Williams liked to call her lovingly because of the strength of her personality—always had some kind of fund-raiser going, Flavin was often pulled into the world of the DiMaggios. He turned out to be the ideal master of ceremonies for any number of events, including one held at the rather posh Kittansett country club that Dominic belongs to on Massachusetts' south shore. (DiMaggio, he noted, was one of only two Dominics actually permitted on the sacred grass there—and, by the way, he added, the other Dominic was the man whose job it was to cut the grass.)

Flavin had become over the years something of an authority on the life of Dominic DiMaggio, so one day when he was in the San Francisco area, he paid a visit to the house at 2047 Taylor Street where the DiMaggios had grown up. He was let in by two young women who lived there, and Flavin was shocked to discover that they did not know whose home it had been or what its cultural value was. He called Dominic on his cell phone, and Dominic narrated a guided tour, sending Flavin from room to room, until at last he reached the tiny room, the last bedroom on the far right, the historic site where Vince, Joe, and Dominic had all slept as boys.

◻

The game plan for the car trip south to visit Ted was this: They would gather at Dominic's house in Marion on Saturday, October 20, 2001, and then would drive first to

Philadelphia, where Dominic was to be the guest of the Philadelphia Athletics Historical Society. Years ago the Athletics had played in Philadelphia, before moving to Kansas City in 1955, where they became the Kansas City Athletics and in time failed, before moving on to Oakland where they still reside and are known as the Oakland Athletics. That the Philly fans were going to get Pesky and Flavin as well was a considerable bonus. (Flavin was going to read "Teddy at the Bat," his own version of Ernest Lawrence Thayer's classic 1888 poem "Casey at the Bat"; in the revised version, Ted replaced Casey and naturally did not let down the Boston/Mudville fans.)

Flavin and DiMaggio, sharing the driving, sat up front, and Pesky, sharing the talking, sat in back. They talked about players they had liked and players they had feared. Pesky said Spud Chandler, the Yankees pitcher, was tough. "God, he was mean. He'd hit you in the ass, just for the sheer pleasure of it. It was like it made him feel good. I had shined his shoes when he had pitched out in the Coast League. It was as if he had some personal thing against me, as if he was insulted by my being in the big leagues. He was the worst tipper in the Pacific Coast League, by the way. In 1942, which was my first year in Boston, we were playing the Yankees, and he was pitching. Ted used to like to get Bobby and me, and sometimes Dom, and take us where we could watch the opposing pitcher warm up to see what he had—in those days they warmed up right in front of the dugout. So we were standing there, watching Chandler, who had a very tough sinkerball, and Jack Malaney of the old *Boston Post* came up to us. And he said, 'Pesky, you don't have a hit off Chandler this season. You're 0 for 14 against him.' And Ted said, 'That's right, Needle. You're always trying to pull the ball against him. He throws a heavy ball—you can't pull it. Needle, I can't pull him, and I'm a foot taller than you and about forty pounds heavier. You have to go with the pitch.' So we get to the bottom of the eighth inning, the score is 1–1, and our catcher gets to first, and Dom doubles, and we have men on second and third, and first is open. So I come up. Bill Dickey is catching, and he goes out to the mound to talk to Chandler. And before I get to the plate Ted takes me aside and says, 'Needle, that's Spud Chandler out there, and he throws a heavy ball. And he is not going to walk you to get to me. So you're going to get a pitch to hit. Don't try and pull it.' It's almost sixty years later and I can still hear him telling me that, that Spud Chandler is not going to walk me to get to him. And I get up, and I take a couple pitches, and I get the sinker and slap it to left, and two runs score. I'm on first and Chandler is going crazy, it's apparently very personal with him—just screaming at me, 'I'll stick one in your ear, you little shit. I'll get you.' Ted is standing at the plate, just grinning away. Ted steps in, and Chandler is still screaming at me, '*You little shit, I'll get you!*' And it's like he's forgotten Ted is the hitter. He finally pitches to Ted, and Ted hits a rocket to right field. Home run! And Ted comes in to the dugout, and he's saying where is our horn-nosed little shortstop—'Didn't I tell you about Chandler? Didn't I tell you? Chandler was so mad at you, he forgot I was the next hitter.'"

As they neared Philly, Dominic was saying that he was rather puzzled as to why he had been invited there. Yes, he had been close to Jimmie Foxx, the superlative Athletics slugger who had played for Boston from 1936 to 1942, and they had roomed together for a time. And, in an unusual feat for one of the younger players, Dominic had even managed to forge a genuine friendship with the great Lefty Grove, who had started his career, like Foxx, in 1925 with the Athletics and had come to Boston in 1934 when Athletics owner and manager Connie Mack was selling off his best players due to financial difficulties. Lefty was a hard man, known as much for his misanthropy as for his brilliant pitching, someone who was very tough on his teammates, famous for ripping off his uniform, sending the buttons flying in all directions, if anyone playing behind him made an error and cost him a victory.

Dominic's relationship with Grove did not start well. When Dom joined the Red Sox in the spring of 1940, Johnny Orlando, the clubhouse boy, brought him around the locker room and introduced him to everyone. "The only two who weren't there were Jimmie Foxx and Lefty Grove," recalled Dominic, "but pretty soon Foxx shows up and sticks out his hand and says, 'Welcome aboard, kid.' But then Grove comes by and walks right by me and doesn't say a thing. And I'd heard that he was quite temperamental and so for two weeks we didn't speak. Every day it seemed we were in the elevator together, but we didn't talk. Not a word was said. And I was thinking, I'm a rookie, and rookies don't speak unless they're spoken to. Especially to Lefty Grove. So then a friend of mine from Boston came down, and said, 'What's this, I hear you don't talk to Lefty Grove?' And I said, 'You've got it all wrong, Grove doesn't speak to me. I'm the rookie—I can't just go up to him and call him Lefty and start talking to him.'" The next day when Dominic was returning to the team hotel, he had to pass two rocking chairs on the front porch. Grove was in one and Orlando in the other. Dominic got very nervous. This was going to be a great social test: "My heart is beating terribly, but I get my nerve up, and I say, 'Hello, Lefty,' and he bounds up, grabs me, hugs me, tells Johnny Orlando to sit somewhere else, tells me to sit in Orlando's chair, and we sat and talked for hours. We became fast friends after that. I caught the last ball hit on his three hundredth victory, the last game he pitched. And I think I was one of two players invited to the dinner to celebrate that win—Jimmie Foxx was the other one."

That was about the extent of Dominic's connection to Philadelphia. And Pesky? What connection did he have except for all those hits against the A's? Well, he said, there was the time he almost got into a fight with Al Simmons, the formidable Athletics outfielder. Simmons was Polish, and he had come into this world not as Al Simmons, but as Aloysius Szymanski. In one game Simmons had been riding Pesky mercilessly, calling him a dumb Polack, which infuriated Pesky, because he was a Croat, not a Pole, and who was Simmons to tell him he was dumb anyway? Was Simmons that much smarter than Pesky? Pesky, the most combative of the four teammates, surely because he was the smallest, was the most likely to get in an on-field fight. He started screaming back at Simmons that he was not Polish, not a Polack, and not a dumb Polack, but he was a Croat, and a smart Croat at that. He would damn well fight Al Simmons right then and there, but Simmons started laughing and yelled back, "Me fight you? You little son of a bitch. What a waste of my time. I'll send the batboy out, and he'll beat the shit out of you."

The conversation in the car, driving south through New England was wonderful, Flavin thought, unself-conscious and unexpurgated. They were a little sad that Bobby was not with them, but without Bobby they did not have to be quite so careful about their language. Bobby never swore. That led to a discussion about the odd pairing of Bobby and Ted, quite possibly the most blasphemous player of all time. It was fascinating, they thought, the way Ted had sought comfort in Bobby, knowing that Bobby could handle situations that he, Ted, could not. The road for Bobby, so secure within himself, was always straight and smooth. By contrast the road for Ted was full of bends and was *always* rough. And thus, even when it momentarily became smooth, Ted would do something to make it bumpy; if there were no obstacles ahead, he might well create some, and if they were small, he was entirely capable of making them larger.

Flavin, sitting with these two older men, was impressed by how much of the past they still remembered, as if it had all taken place just yesterday, instead of more than 50 years ago. "John," Dominic asked Pesky at one point, "do you remember the play we used to pull?" Flavin asked what that was, and they told him. In those days Dominic, who had greater speed than Pesky, was the leadoff man, and Pesky, who had great bat control, was second in the lineup, with Ted generally batting third. Sometimes when Dominic got on first, he and Pesky would work their own play: Pesky would rub his nose, which meant he would either bunt or try the hit-and-run. On this play, though, Dominic would not stop at second, but keep going without any hesitation to third—just as the third baseman was coming in, and the defense was concentrating on Pesky. They ran it flawlessly for a time, and it worked as long as they did not overdo it. Of the catchers around the league only Buddy Rosar of the A's caught on. In 1946, that golden year when everything went so well, and Pesky again led the league in hits and Dominic hit .316, they used it with great success. "But then we got a little too cocky and we talked about it, and one of the Boston sportswriters wrote something about it," Dominic recalled. "Anyway, we came into Yankee Stadium. It was Bill Dickey's last year. Yogi [Berra] was just coming up, I think. And I'm on first, and John goes to his nose. And I take off, and I go roaring into third base, sure I'm safe. And there's Bill

Dickey over the bag, holding the ball and tagging me out. 'Got you,' he said, and I asked him how he knew, and he said, 'I read the papers too.' "

◻

The event in Philly went well. More than 500 people turned out to greet them, as well as some old-time ballplayers, including Eddie Joost, who played shortstop for the A's for almost a decade, Mickey Vernon, a wondrous line drive hitter who spent most of his career with Washington, Bobby Shantz, one of the first pitchers to specialize as a reliever, and Bill Werber, an infielder who was by then 93. Werber once tangled with Dominic in spring training, more than 60 years ago, when Dominic had dropped a bunt and beat the throw to first for a hit. Werber, who was playing deep at third, thought Dominic was trying to show him up, so he started shouting at him, neither man backing down, and there was almost a fight. When Dominic spotted Werber at the Philadelphia event, he wondered if there would still be a bit of the old grudge in the air; was this 93-year-old, after all these years, going to try to settle the score with an 84-year-old? "Dom Di-Maggio offered to punch me in the nose that day, but I politely declined the offer," Werber told the audience. So, mercifully, it was all in the past. Everyone was impressed by the size of the crowd. "If we could have drawn like that in the old days, the A's would still be here," one fan said. Dominic and John signed autographs the first night, and the next morning they spoke, and Flavin did his reading. When they left town, the three of them were very happy. "We took Philly by storm," Dominic said.

JOHN PESKY

THREE

RUTH AND JOHN PESKY

W hen they had left Philadelphia, Dominic was driving, and John was sleeping in the backseat, but, after 70 miles or so, they passed through a small city, and John briefly woke up. "Where are we?" he asked, and Flavin told him they were in Lancaster, Pennsylvania. "Oh my God," Pesky said, "I used to manage here. Amish country. Very nice people. Detroit organization. Class A." Then came a quick list of some of the players he had managed who had gone up the ladder in baseball. That seemed quite in keeping with the trip, because wherever they went John Pesky had already been there at one time or another, always in a baseball uniform. So many towns and cities, forming a special map, John Pesky's own private United States of Baseball.

After his career as a major leaguer was over, he had gone to Denver, then a Yankee farm club, in 1955, coaching and playing a little under Ralph Houk, who had been the Yankees' backup catcher and was New York's manager-in-waiting. Then, in 1956, Pesky went to Durham, North Carolina, Class B, managing the one-day-to-be-famous Durham Bulls; then to Birmingham, Alabama, in 1957; to Lancaster in 1958; to Knoxville in 1959; to Victoria in the Texas League in 1960. (Victoria was remembered principally because its owner was "one of the nicest men I ever worked for," but his name temporarily escaped Pesky in the overload of names in his personal Hall of Fame.) Then back to the Red Sox organization, managing in Seattle in 1961 and 1962. Seattle was a minor league team in those years, and it was maybe the best job he ever had— wonderful, young players, many of them ready to go to the majors. He returned to Boston in 1963, to manage briefly but not happily, because he and Pinky Higgins, the former Boston third baseman who had preceded Pesky in the infield and had then managed and gone upstairs to the front office (and who struggled with serious alcohol problems), never saw eye to eye. "Everyone else wants to manage in the majors, but I would have been much happier staying in Seattle and managing there. It was an ideal situation—the talent level is very good and the players still listen to you," Pesky said. Then over to the Pirates, three years coaching there, wonderful years, among the best ballplayers he ever dealt with, particularly the talented young slugger Willie Stargell, born two years before Pesky broke in with Boston. (To this day, when Pesky spots a young player he likes not just as a player but as a man, he uses Stargell as his measuring rod, the requisite qualities being uncommon inner strength and human richness.) Actually, Pesky thought there were a great many special men there, including Bob Friend, Bill Virdon, and, of course, Roberto Clemente.

In 1968 Pesky managed the Pirates' farm team in Columbus, Ohio, then he went back to Boston, under different management, and some six years working in the broadcast booth—a job, strangely enough, that he did not like very much, probably, his friends thought, because it forced him to be critical of ballplayers in public on occasion. What became clear, listening to Pesky's odyssey, was that he was better in the minors than in the majors, better with young players who wanted to learn than with veterans, and that as baseball changed over the years, becoming a harder and edgier universe, with more and more of an emphasis on the money, he was probably too nice a man to hold one of the managing jobs at the top.

There was about John Michael Pesky, the 82-year-old man

in the backseat, the sense of the perpetual ingénue, the boy who had started his life in a baseball uniform almost 70 years earlier, had spent a lifetime in that uniform, and had somehow remained, though he had long since grown to manhood, still a boy. He had been a local icon in Boston for more than 60 years, but in some important way he remained utterly unchanged, still very much the kid living out his dream, wary that someone might wake him up and take it all away. There was no artifice to him, no arrogance; unlike so many older ballplayers he never became hard and grizzled, but instead remained kind, caring, almost innocent. With so many ballplayers the sweetest moments come when they are still so young, and they spend long decades afterwards wondering why life is never again quite so rewarding; in addition, many of the old-timers cannot get over the fact that today's ballplayers make more in one *game* than they made in an entire season. But Pesky was in no way disappointed with his life during or after the major leagues.

These days when a friend called the house and asked to speak to The Legend, Ruth Pesky will note, amused by it all, "There are no legends here." They had been married for 56 years and many of their friends were people they had known back in the '40s. Sixty years after making the big club for the first time, he still worked for the Red Sox, which had first employed him in 1942. He still ate breakfast most mornings with the same group of men who were his neighbors in Lynn and Swampscott; they began, first things first, by dissecting what had happened to the Red Sox on the previous day, a subject on which John was involuntarily the leading expert. The men were his pals, and they all spoke the same easy language; their friendships had evolved out of a love of the same baseball team and the myriad disappointments of following that team over so many decades of heartbreak. (My friend Marty Nolan, the former editorial page editor of the *Boston Globe*, once famously described the pain that came with being a Red Sox fan: "They killed my father, and now they're coming after me.")

There was also, because he was such a local celebrity, the annual Pesky Dinner, which was held annually in Lynn, and it celebrated the fact that Johnny Pesky had remained throughout the years, Johnny Pesky. The official title, fittingly enough, was The Friendship Dinner, and it was one of the major time-warp occasions in America, for the early 1950s still reigned at the Pesky Dinner. It was all male (if there were women present, they were serving food, as one regular said); many of the men smoked, including the honoree; they were all in some way or another his pals, for John had lots of friends, and even more pals, people who knew him in a more transitory way, but greatly valued their connection to him, the fact that they knew and were close to a beloved big league ballplayer, and that he always knew who they were and never came on like a big star.

The Friendship Dinner started back when John was still playing and a few of his neighbors would take him out to dinner the night before he left for spring training. The first time it happened there were eight or ten of them. They went to a local restaurant, had steaks, and then stayed on for a few drinks. It had turned out to be an unusually warm and affectionate evening, and someone said at the end, Hey, we ought to do this every year. John, loving it, protested that No, they shouldn't, that it was all too much fuss. But that made his pals even more determined to turn it into an annual event. That is, it would be an annual event if it worked, and if it didn't it would die out of its own accord. Of course it worked, and it had begun to grow, a few more people attending each year, as other friends heard about it and wanted in. Instead of eight friends, there were soon a dozen, and then 20, and then one day over 100, and ever larger venues were needed to hold everyone. Though there were still no women present, it was not in any way a stag party, there was nothing smutty about it—there was always a monsignor present. Rather, it was like an old-fashioned, father-son sports banquet. Often other Red Sox players showed up, and there were a number of years when Ted had come.

In 2002, the fiftieth anniversary of the John Pesky Dinner was held, and boys who had once come with their fathers, wide-eyed and excited to meet Johnny Pesky, now came with their sons. People got up and made speeches, and then Johnny himself spoke, and though he was not a great public speaker, those speeches were very much like the man himself: warm and loving and absolutely without guile or meanness. By this point the Friendship Dinner had become perilously close to a state occasion; there had been a brief attempt to move it from Lynn, right near where John lived on the outskirts of Boston, to someplace more chic in Boston proper. But that move was quickly quashed—surely at such a restaurant there would be a ban on smoking, especially smoking cigars. Among other reasons to keep it in Lynn was the fact that Ruth Hickey Pesky was a Lynn girl. They had been married for more than 50 years; they had first met while both were serving in the Navy in Atlanta. Ruth Hickey thought that John was vain and a fathead when she first met him. She quickly changed that judgment, but, it is important to note, *never let him forget it*. So the dinner would remain at a simpler place in Lynn; Johnny was not going to try for an upgrade.

Pesky, though the only one of the four teammates who played for other teams, was in some ways the most enduring member of the Boston cast, at various times player, coach, manager, and announcer, and, perhaps more important, a friend to multiple generations of the city's players, writers, trainers, and fans. It was hard to think of him in street clothes, only in a uniform, and a Boston uniform at that. Once, after their playing careers were over, Dom DiMaggio was doing well with his manufacturing company, and, knowing that the Red Sox were not paying John very well, offered him a job with his company. Pesky thought about it—it would be a lot more money, and it might make things easier down the road—but in the end he turned it down. "Dom, I couldn't love my own brothers

more than I love you, and I want to thank you, but I'm a baseball man, and it's all I'll ever be. It's all I know," he told his old
teammate. "I'll wear the uniform until I die, and then they'll
probably have to cut it off me." In 2002 he was still going to
Fenway Park early every day when the Red Sox were playing
at home, hitting fungos to men who might well be his grand-
children.

Ted Williams had always watched out for Pesky from a dis-
tance, and in the spring of 1997, when, in a bizarre and much-
criticized front-office move, the Red Sox management kicked
Pesky out of the dugout and forced him to turn in his uniform,
Ted made a number of phone calls to important people in
Boston, volubly expressing his displeasure with the decision. In
February 2002 the Red Sox were sold, and one of the first
things the new principal owner, John Henry, did was restore
Pesky to his uniform and his coaching duties—thus showing
that he knew more about Boston baseball history than general
manager Dan Duquette, who was himself let go in the change
of ownership. Duquette was certainly smart, but his personnel
moves always seemed more than a little elephantine. It was almost as if his strategy was designed to separate himself from the
team's rich history and lore, as if the past was more of a burden
than an enhancement, and that in order to build for the future,
he had to destroy the past.

◻

J acob Paveskovich, John's father, arrived in this country around 1912 from what was then the Austro-Hungarian empire, along with some friends of his, including the grandfather of Mickey Lolich, who later was a pitching star for the Detroit Tigers in the 1968 World Series. Jacob Paveskovich had served with the Austro-Hungarian Navy right before World War One. During World War Two, John was rather quickly promoted to officer in one of the Navy's sped-up programs, and Jacob was enormously impressed. "John, do you know how long it took me to get what you got in the old country, to become an officer?" he asked his son when the latter came home in his officer's uniform. "No," John said. "Ten or twelve years. And you got it in under two years." "Pop," John said, "we're not in the old country—we're in the new country." "Yes," Jacob said and he smiled, "you're right, John—we're not in the old country."

His father had taken whatever work he could get when he arrived in America, at first going west to Oregon with his pals to work in the logging camps. He ended up at a sawmill in Portland, cutting timber, and had settled in a house in a rough section of Portland referred to as Slabtown, named for the leftover slabs of wood that the mill workers used for heating and cooking. (Because there were so many people of Slavic descent who lived in the area, many later-day Portland residents believed the nickname reflected East European ethnicity— a corruption of Slavtown—rather than pieces of wood.) The sawmill was a tough place to work, his son remembered, but it paid the mortgage. "Maybe he made $15 a week—maybe a little more," John recalled. "But not much more. But we had our house, and there was always enough food on the table." There were six children, three boys and three girls. John was fifth in the birth order, and was thus allowed a little more freedom than his older siblings. Their home, like that of many immigrants, was strict, and everyone had to work. "The rule of the house was very simple," John said. "If you didn't work for it, you didn't get it." There was a tall oak tree across the street, and John's mother, Maria, would periodically cut branches off it, whittle them down for switches, and place them throughout her house as warnings for her children that they had better behave. John would try to find them and get rid of them.

When John was young, one of his jobs was delivering food from a local grocery store, and one of his customers was a family living in a rural area called Minton. The family had some chickens and a handsome rooster that John quite admired. One day, when no one was home, he chased the rooster for about 20 minutes, finally captured him, and brought him home to keep as a pet. His mother was not amused. "Where did you get it?" she asked. John told her the truth, that the rooster was now a pet. No, he was not going to keep it, she explained. He was going to take the rooster right back to the family, and he was going to apologize. "You have to understand, John," she said, "that those people need the rooster. This is not a pet."

The Paveskovich family lived on 20th Street, and Vaughn Street Ballpark, the Portland stadium, was at 24th Street. The neighborhood kids were drawn to it like a magnet. An older man named Rocky Benevento was the groundskeeper at the park and, blessedly, he was one of those rare men in such a job who did not feel that his first order of business each day was to chase away the neighborhood kids. Instead he let them play on the field whenever the Beavers were on the road, and he let them help with his chores—was there a greater honor? When John Paveskovich was about 12, he got his first job at the ballpark, which was keeping the bullpens clean by sweeping them out and patting down the dirt. In his mind it was the best job any kid had in the entire state of Oregon. From there he eventually graduated to clubhouse boy, a job in which he got to meet the visiting ballplayers and made as much as $10 a week in tips. The Pacific Coast League, thanks to the good weather, had a very long season. Visiting teams stayed in a city for a week—they traveled by train on Sunday night, Monday was an off-day, and thereafter they played every day, ending the week with a mandatory doubleheader. That minimized travel costs. Thus, as the clubhouse boy, John got to know the visiting players rather well. Sometimes barnstorming black teams would come to town, and John remembered when Satchel Paige and Josh Gibson, the great stars of the Negro League, would come in, and how talented they were. At a certain point during each game, usually in the third inning, John remembered, Satchel would wave to his teammates, who would all sit down, and then Josh Gibson would catch behind the plate, sitting in a rocking chair—just to let everyone know how good Satch was.

By this time Pesky was himself playing a lot of ball in the city leagues and those that operated out of nearby towns. He was good, although his size seemed to work against him, and he was not sure he was going to make it as a pro. In the summer of 1937 he was playing for a Bend, Oregon, sawmill team, working in the mill during the day and playing for the company team at night. One day the ballclub's manager came by, saw him at work, and was made nervous. Not wanting Bend's prize shortstop to lose a finger, he pulled him off the job and switched him to a less dangerous one, a measure of courtesy never in all those years afforded to his father, the breadwinner of a large family. Jacob's fingers, in this new world, were not nearly as precious as those of his 16-year-old son.

Back in Portland, John kept working as the clubhouse boy, because he loved to be around the game, to see the players coming through, especially the ones he knew were ticketed for the big leagues. He had by then already become Johnny Pesky, the name Paveskovich having been judged too long for a box-score by the local sportswriters. Since he was a pesky hitter, a little guy who slapped the ball around, the new name seemed especially appropriate. His name started going into sports stories as Pesky, and then people started using it all the time. He had become, in a uniquely American way, and almost with no choice in the matter, Johnny Pesky.

He made it his legal name in 1947. His mother had been upset when he changed his name legally, fearing that he was ashamed of his name. "Ma, I'm not ashamed, but we're in America now," he had said, but she was still uneasy with it. But then he noted that as he began to do well, she became something of a local celebrity as well, the mother of Johnny Pesky of the Red Sox, and she had begun to like it, especially when she went to church on Sunday and people would treat her with great respect, complete strangers coming up to her, saying, *Good morning, Mrs. Pesky. How are you today?*

In 1938, when he was still 18, several scouts began to show interest in him. The Yankees did, so did the St. Louis Cardinals, and the Cleveland Indians, and of course, the Red Sox. Scouting was not exactly a science in those days and there was a certain hit-or-miss quality to it. He remembered that in 1938 he was playing for a team in Silverton, about 30 miles from Portland; it was a double-elimination tournament and there was a scout there from the Cards, a big, powerful guy. John was working as a groundskeeper, dragging the field and outlining the batter's box, as well as playing. After he finished the scout came over to him and asked, "Is Silverton playing tonight?" Pesky said yes, they were. "I hear they've got some good young ballplayers," said the scout. Pesky said, yes, they did, and he mentioned the team's second baseman, Don Kirsch. The man looked more closely at Pesky, who was stripped to the waist. "You play?" he asked, and Pesky said yes, he did. "What's your name?" he asked, and Pesky told him. "Oh Christ, I'm supposed to see you play tonight." That night Pesky got a bunch of hits and after the third day the Cardinal scout said he was interested in him and asked if anyone else was as well. Pesky told him that the Red Sox were. "I like what I see," the Cardinal scout said, "and I'm going to offer you $1,500 to sign."

But it was never just about money. Pesky's older brothers and sisters did not think the money was the critical issue, and his parents, new to this country, wanted to do things the right way, the way Americans did. They were not baseball fans, at least not yet. Jacob's idea of sports was boccie, which he played for a few hours on Friday afternoons with some of his pals from the old country, with everybody drinking homemade wine. But John's parents were willing to make their adjustments to America; if this was what John wanted—and his brothers and sisters all said it was a very good thing—then so be it. Playing sports in school, after all, had kept him out of trouble. Of all the scouts, the one Mrs. Paveskovich preferred was the Boston representative, a man named Ernie Johnson, because he seemed to be interested in the entire family. Johnson visited the Paveskovich home two or three times, and, faithful to the tricks of the trade, he always brought presents: flowers for Maria and a bottle of I. W. Harper bourbon for Jacob.

It was very much a family decision: One of John's older brothers did the interpreting. Johnson was offering only $500, a third of the Cardinal offer. John had said he preferred the Cardinal offer. "No, John," his mother said, "you go to Boston. Mr. Johnson will take care of you. I know he will. He will look out for you." Ernie Johnson nodded his head sagely at the right moment, as if the first thing on his agenda when he got up in the morning for the next two years was going to be keeping an eye out for John Pesky, checking in regularly with his manager to see how he was doing. "I was somewhat more dubious about that," John remembered. "I thought he would be on to his next scouting assignment, instead of taking care of me, that I would be more or less forgotten as he went to some other distant place, charming some other kid's immigrant parents, and I must have showed it, so he upped his offer." "I'll tell you what," Johnson said. "I'll give you an additional $1,000 if you stay in the organization two years."

So in the spring of 1939, John Pesky found himself leaving Oregon for the first time in his life, and heading east to Rocky Mount, North Carolina, Class B, the Piedmont League. The salary was $150 a month, easy to live on because there was a little meal money, and so he managed to send home about $50 a month. He had no illusions that he would make the big leagues. His dream was to be good enough to make it back to the Pacific Coast League, where he would sometimes be able to play in front of old friends, and perhaps even play for the hometown Beavers. In Rocky Mount, it was his good fortune to have as his manager Heinie Manush, a great hitter himself, with 17 years in the big leagues and a career .330 batting average; he had led the American League in hitting in 1926, batting .378. Manush, then 37 years old, was, John thought, a wonderful man, the perfect teacher for young, eager baseball players; he became something of a role model and the kindnesses—and tolerance—Pesky would eventually bestow on the young minor league players he managed were similar to those Manush showed him.

The first two weeks at Rocky Mount were chaotic as Manush attempted to sort through all these young men who had been sent to him, trying to figure out who was actually a ballplayer and who was not. It was soon apparent that John Pesky was a real ballplayer, someone with remarkable instincts for the game, a kid who always seemed to make contact with the ball. Manush did not like his swing, though. John was small, and his body was still forming—it was not yet very muscular— but, eager to make it as a pro, he was trying to swing as if he were a power hitter. Manush did not say anything to Pesky for almost two weeks, in order not to rush him, but finally when John was playing some pepper games—something he was very good at—Manush came over and said, "You know John, if you keep holding your bat at the end, the way you're doing now, when you get to the majors, they'll knock the bat out of your hand." "Hey, Heinie," Pesky answered, "I'm strong, they won't do that." But Manush said quite gently, "John, I know you're strong, but you'll get to the majors, and they're strong too, and they throw 90 miles an hour, and you're not *that* strong, and they *will* knock the bat out of your hand. Look, you have good bat control. You see the ball very well. You make contact well. I want you to try this: I want you to choke up just a little. You'll have better bat control. You won't lose any real power because you're not a power hitter. That won't be your job. Your job will be to get on base." Then he added, "John, I want you to think of this: When you're about to pick up a heavy piece of wood, where do you reach for it?" Pesky answered the center. "Why?" Manush asked, and then answered his own question. "Because you have more control over it—it's harder if you pick it up from the end. It's the same with a bat." He pointed out that when they played pepper games—informal games where you tried to hit the ball as quickly as you could to other infielders gathered around—no one was better at it than Pesky. Manush added, "Johnny, one of the reasons you're so good at pepper games is because you choke up on the bat when you play them, and when you do that your bat control is marvelous."

So Pesky tried choking up a little, and he *did* have better bat control. Manush also taught him to stand a little closer to the plate, but a little farther back in the batter's box. That was the making of Johnny Pesky, the skilled spray hitter. Even more important, Manush gave him the most crucial advice for a young ballplayer: Accept who you are, maximize your strengths, minimize your weaknesses. If you don't have size, don't try to fake it and play like you're a power hitter. "John," he said, "don't try and be what you're not." Pesky later decided that Manush had simply reinforced what Wade Williams, his high-school coach in Portland, had always taught him. Williams, the coach at Lincoln High, had been a very good baseball man, if a little gruff, as men of that generation often were. He had pushed Pesky, who barely weighed 150 pounds, to be a line drive hitter, and not to be seduced by the school's short fence in right field, which often encouraged limited hitters to think they were power hitters. Pesky had been a little cocky at first, sure he could drive the ball like a true power hitter, but Williams convinced him that his future was in contact, and in line drives, and that it was a mistake to try and muscle the ball. Now here was Manush telling him the same thing.

Pesky had a very good year at Rocky Mount, hitting .325. Manush, knowing that Boston's shortstop, Joe Cronin, was 33 and coming to the end of his playing days, suggested that Pesky join the Red Sox for the tail end of the 1940 season. "I want Cronin to take a look at you," he said. "I want you up in Boston." But Pesky, not knowing how the organizational game was played, not realizing that this was a great break, said he was tired and more than a little homesick. He simply wanted to go back home to Portland once the season was over. "If I had known then what I knew later, I'd have gone in a second. But I was just a kid, so I went home." "Okay, Pacific Coast League," Manush said, using his nickname for him. "Whatever you want." But at least the promised $1,000 bonus from the Red Sox, due if he lasted two years, arrived early, at the end of the first year.

The next year, 1941, Pesky knew he was ready for the AA Louisville Colonels, the Red Sox's top farm club, but he assumed that no matter how well he did in Louisville, the organization would send him down early in the season to Scranton, the team's A-ball club, or even a notch lower. There were prejudices against moving players up too quickly, especially players who were not that big, and did not necessarily look like big league players, and there was a debate in the organization about whether the 21-year-old Pesky was moving up in the farm system too quickly. Bill Burwell, the Louisville manager, wanted to slow his progress and give him another year or two in the minors, but Billy Evans, a former umpire and former Cleveland Indians general manager who was then heading the Red Sox farm system, watched him play and thought he could obviously hit AA pitching. Pesky was by now a committed contact hitter—he had accepted Manush's teaching as gospel, for the truth of it was in the numbers he was posting. Evans thought that given this style of contact hitting, Pesky would hit equally well in the majors; he believed as well that Pesky's speed would add something defensively to the infield, now that Joe Cronin was nearing the end of his career. Pesky spent the year in Louisville, again hitting .325, again leading the league in hits, and was voted American Association MVP, so it was decided that he was ready for the big club in 1942.

That winter he received his first big league contract in the mail. It called for him to be paid $4,000 for the coming year with Boston. Young and green as he was, even John Pesky knew that wasn't enough. He decided he wanted $5,000, though his older brother Anthony told him to sign the contract and not make any trouble. "Don't make them mad at you, John," he warned. But John sent the contract back, asking for $1,000 more, and a week later the same contract, offering the same $4,000, arrived in the mail, accompanied by a note from the Red Sox general manager, Eddie Collins, a Hall of Fame second baseman. It said that they did not know if he could play in the big leagues, so John signed and went to spring training with the big league club. He was fighting for a place in the infield with another would-be rookie named Eddie Pellagrini, who had played for San Diego. At the end of spring training, Cronin sent Pellagrini to Louisville, but he did not tell Pesky he had made the club. Then, when the team was on its way north, the Red Sox played an exhibition game against the Cincinnati Reds. Johnny Vander Meer, who was one of the toughest pitchers in the game—he threw back-to-back no-hitters in 1938 and led the National League in strikeouts in 1941—was pitching for the Reds. Pesky hit a triple to right center. After the game Cronin came over to him and said, "Kid, you just made the ball club." It all came together so easily: In his rookie season Pesky hit .331, second in the A.L. only to Williams' .356, and he once again led the league, this time the American League, in hits.

One night at the very end of the first season, he was told to go see Eddie Collins after the game. While Ted waited for him—they were going for a steak dinner that night—he went to see Collins, who handed him an envelope. "Mr. Yawkey wanted you to have this," Collins said, referring to the team owner. There was a check for $5,000 in it. Collins said that Pesky had been a good boy, had played well, and had not given them any trouble. Pesky was amazed. He showed the check to Ted, who told him to send it to his parents immediately, which he was going to do anyway, and they bought a house. It is the house where his brother Anthony still lives.

BOBBY DOERR

FOUR

TED WILLIAMS AND BOBBY DOERR,
ROGUE RIVER, OREGON, 1987

A s they drove south, Dick Flavin, who had been a speaker at the Pesky Dinner several times and quite loved the now almost archaic sense of tradition it represented, started thinking that at the next dinner they should play a home video featuring Ted Williams and Bobby Doerr, the two of them arguing about hitting in the middle of a fishing trip on the Rogue River in 1987. It was vintage Williams, Flavin thought, the man as he really was—so alive, argumentative, and dominating. It would be a wonderful way of bringing Ted to life in that room. For sure, they would have to bleep out a number of words, but other than that it would be perfect for the Pesky Dinner, a way of showing the friendship these men shared.

The video captured a wonderful moment, one of many chapters in the 60-year debate between Williams and Doerr over hitting. Whenever the subject arose, Doerr became, in Ted's words, "that goddamn Bobby Doerr," as in, "I can't teach that goddamn Bobby Doerr anything about hitting. I don't know what's wrong with him. He just won't listen." The marathon debate had begun when they were young; even then Ted was the most passionate of hitters, and hitting was nothing less than a science for him. No one studied it as diligently as he did, and he never put comparable energy into, say, the science of fielding. Ted was in a class apart in the way he constantly scrutinized pitchers ("dumb by breed") and what they threw and when they threw it. In the pre-computerized age, everything was categorized and everything was stored away. As such, he was rarely surprised by what pitchers threw; if anyone was surprised, it was likely to be the pitcher. He was immensely frustrated by the fact that Doerr, a very good natural hitter, was not as passionate about the subject as he was.

There were all too many games when Ted would ask Bobby what kind of pitch he had just hit, and Bobby would say that he did not know, he had just gone up there and hit the ball. Ted would say, Goddamn it! How could Bobby Doerr not goddamn know what he had swung at? And then Bobby would try to explain the difference between being a middle infielder, where you were in on every play or at least had to be ready to be in on every play, and being an outfielder, where the pressures were far less intense. Being a middle infielder drained you. Well, an answer like that was pure bullshit, in the loudly expressed opinion of Theodore Samuel Williams, but if Bobby Doerr wanted to go through life being a goddamn .280 hitter, instead of a .300 hitter, he had Ted Williams' permission to do it. (Actually, Doerr turned out to be a career .288 hitter.) All of their teammates knew of the debate, had witnessed it countless times, and could years later quote back Ted's side, if not Bobby's, which had often been drowned out.

What none of them knew, or at least knew at the time, was that Bobby Doerr was one of the few people who could correct Ted when he slipped out of synch with his own swing. Periodically, Doerr noticed, Ted would go on a bit of a long ball binge, hungering for home runs instead of just going up there and swinging naturally. When that happened, he tended to drop his hands just before he started his swing, but he did not bring them back up as he normally would, and it would throw the swing off. If anyone else tried to talk to Ted about his swing, he tended to explode, but Bobby could, though he had to do it in private. It all had to be done very deftly, phrased carefully, a loving suggestion, never a criticism. Even so, the fact that Ted would listen to Bobby reflected the unique trust he had in him. Doerr was, in fact, very astute about Williams as a hitter. For instance, in 1941, the year Ted hit .406, Bobby noticed that he had made a slight adaptation in his swing because he had chipped a bone in his right ankle during spring training. Every day Williams would have it wrapped, and he favored the ankle throughout the season. Because of that, Bobby believed that Williams as a left-handed hitter was favoring his right or front foot and staying back a little more when he swung and so he hit an inordinate number of sinking line drives just past the second baseman into right field.

At the crux of their ongoing debate, even more than Ted's feeling that Bobby should be more passionate, was the fact that Ted believed, actually he *knew*, that you should always swing slightly up, as in, *Well, of course, you should swing slightly up because the goddamn pitchers' mound, as everyone who knows anything at all about baseball except for Bobby Doerr knows, is 15 inches higher than the plate.* (It was lowered to ten inches after the 1968 season when pitchers appeared to be overpowering hitters and the MVPs in both leagues, Bob Gibson and Denny McLain, were pitchers.) What was even worse, even more trying, was that he, Ted Williams—the last man to hit .400 in a season, as he and everyone else knew, and therefore he did not have to mention the fact—had been trying to explain this simple fact to Bobby

Doerr for all those years and Doerr still did not listen, still insisted on that stupid, level swing of his. All that Doerr would do is answer that his swing worked for him. Which was obviously a terrible and inadequate answer. Well then, maybe someone else could do something about Bobby Doerr, because he, Ted Williams, was going to wash his hands of Bobby and that sorry flat swing.

But Ted could never quite bring himself to let the matter drop, as the video Flavin wanted to play proved. Ted had called Bobby that year and asked how the steelhead fishing was out in Illahe, Oregon, where the Doerrs had a rustic home. Bobby said it was good, or at least it was with the smaller steelheads. He invited Ted to come out and see for himself. Steelheads, it should be noted, are anadromous rainbow trout, fierce game fish that are born and spawn in freshwater, but live in saltwater. They are more like salmon than trout, and much prized by serious fishermen. Ted was interested in going after the big steelheads; Bobby said that might be more problematic, but that they would give it a shot and go out on the Rogue River, a great river for steelheads and thus something of a fishing paradise. Ted, in time, had shown up, his three marriages by then over, and he was with a wonderful lady named Lou Kaufman, a kind and forgiving person who had moved in and out of his life over the years. She was much admired by most of Ted's old friends and was, by consensus among them, the woman in Ted's life who seemed to understand him best and who could calm him down most readily when one of those instant moments of pure anger had been triggered. She was kind and thoughtful and truly loving—and she seemed, I once thought, when we were all three together for a day back in 1988, as much parent to him as lady-friend.

On this trip Ted was, Bobby thought, quite hyper—really revved up—and as sometimes happened when he was in such a state, he was particularly hard on Lou. Practiced at how to handle this situation, she deflected much of his anger, pretending as if it were not really there. By contrast, Ted was respectful to Monica Doerr, as always, in part because she was Bobby's wife, and in part because she never bought into his baseball fame and whatever right it bestowed on him to be temperamental. She did not treat him as the Great Ted Williams, but just as she would any other friend of Bobby's.

Bobby thought Ted was edgy because several of Bobby's buddies were coming down to fish with them, and Ted was anxious about meeting them, wondering if it would work out all right with these strangers—like a little boy uncertain how he would do with new acquaintances. But then he met them and decided they were okay, and he began to relax. He was loud and voluble nonetheless, and on their second day on the Rogue, he started nicking away at Bobby on the subject of hitting. "You always chopped at the ball," he said. "No, I didn't chop," Doerr countered. "I never understood why you chopped at the ball so much," Ted answered, thus turning the disputed point into a fact. As the argument continued into the third day, they decided to have a hitting clinic, right there on the banks of the Rogue. When they took their morning break, Williams and Doerr, in their grubby fishing clothes, agreed to present their respective arguments. Fortunately for posterity, one of Doerr's friends had a video camera. The other men gathered around, and ground rules were set: five minutes for each man to make his case. First, Ted gave his view of hitting, that the pitcher's mound was up, and so you had to swing slightly up, 12 percent to be exact. (If this was true, Bobby had sometimes teased him, what about curve balls, which broke down? Should they be hit with a 45-degree upswing?) Then it was Bobby's turn—he believed too many hitters swung over the ball precisely because they were swinging up. Patiently and modestly, he laid out his case, while, in the background, Ted tried to distract him, arguing, haranguing, doing everything he could to break Bobby's concentration.

Flavin, watching the video, wondered what it must have been like for other fishermen on the Rogue that day, floating down the river in search of steelheads, and coming upon this loud, boisterous party on the bank, and hearing an overpowering voice echoing up and down the river, and looking up to see a tall, older man wearing baggy old clothes, shouting to everyone and then taking practice baseball swings. Any other fisherman witnessing this must have been utterly puzzled by the scene—*batting practice on the Rogue River during steelhead season?*—and then realizing, even as their boat had swept by and had gone a little farther down the river, what it was all about and that that large, rather voluble man was Ted Williams, yes Ted Williams, holding a riverbank hitting clinic.

Fishing, as much as baseball, had always brought Williams and Doerr together. A couple of neighbors—in particular, a man named Les Cassie, whose own sons weren't much interested in fishing—had taken Williams fishing as a boy, and he had loved it from the first, the solitude of it, the way it enabled him to escape from other pressures at least temporarily, and perhaps most important for Williams, the chance it offered to seek perfection and to excel in yet another arena. Bobby Doerr had also been pulled toward the outdoors since boyhood, and when he had played with the Padres, Les Cook, the team trainer, kept photos of the Rogue posted on his notice board. Cook fished the river in the off-season and often talked with Doerr about how beautiful the river was, and how good the steelhead fishing was there. So when Bobby was 18 years old, still a minor leaguer, he went there with Cook, and he knew from the first day he saw it that he had found an outdoorsman's paradise.

At one point on that trip they were unloading their gear from the boat, when Cook had pointed to a lovely young woman off in the distance and said, "Look, Bobby, that's the schoolteacher right over there." Sixty-six years later Doerr still remembered with singular clarity that day and the exact moment he first saw Monica; it had been windy out and her wonderful red hair was blowing in the wind. Les Cook had already teased Bobby about the young schoolteacher and about how pretty she was. Monica Terpin taught in a nearby one-room schoolhouse and her students were mostly Native Americans. It soon became clear that Doerr had fallen in love not only with the beauty of the land, but with the schoolteacher as well; it was as if she and the land went together. In time, he married the schoolteacher and, borrowing a little money from his father, bought 160 acres there, and for the next 60 years he never really left the area, even in those years when he happily went off to Boston each spring to play baseball.

Bobby Doerr loved Ted Williams. He knew all his faults and loved him just the same. It was a rare thing to go back that far with anyone, let alone a teammate, and to share so much history with him, Doerr believed. As two very young players on the Padres they had bonded first because they both liked going to movie Westerns, especially ones starring Gene Autry or Hoot Gibson. Doerr soon became Ted's confidant, the one person he could always turn to. Later when they were both on the Red Sox, and Williams struggled to deal with fans and the media, and on occasion with some of his older teammates, he and Doerr would often arrive in a city by train and check into the hotel together. Williams, restless and edgy, always high-strung from the pressures that went with being a superstar, from the additional pressures to excel that he put on himself, and, Doerr guessed, from the nature of his emotional wiring, would want to go for a walk—but only with Doerr. If another player wanted to join them, Ted would, more often than not, simply go back to his room. Being close to Ted in those years had given

Doerr a special sense of the pressures that are suffered by a star on a great team. He is the player on whom so much depends, and so the game was absolutely different for him, Doerr decided, than it was for all the other players.

It was a cherished friendship for both of them. But that did not mean it was ever easy. There were going to be wonderful days with Ted, and there were going to be stormy days as well— tempestuous was the word that Bobby used for his friend. There were going to be things Ted did that you simply could not explain to other people who would find the sudden changes in his behavior inexplicable. Sometimes for no apparent reason he would simply explode at you, and it made no difference what you did or said; if you were there when one of those moods hit, then it was simply your bad luck.

That extended to fishing with him whether in Oregon or back in the Florida Keys during the 40-odd years that Ted had a place there. Part of it was that he was always both a perfectionist and purist, as much in his fishing incarnation as in his baseball one. Everyone knew that, including Carl Yastrzemski, the talented ballplayer who had replaced Ted in left field for Boston, two men playing one position for one team from 1939 to 1983 (minus Ted's years in the service). Back when Yaz was still playing, Ted still went to spring training as a hitting instructor. Hearing that Yaz liked to fish, Ted invited him to go fishing. At the appointed hour, Yaz had shown up at the dock where Ted kept his boat, albeit carrying a cooler. "What's in the cooler?" Ted had asked. "Some beer," Yaz had answered. "There's no beer drinking allowed on my boat," Ted said. "Okay—see you, Ted," said Yaz, who turned away and went home. Ted's old teammate, Billy Goodman, who for a time had lived near Ted in Florida, used to warn Doerr about fishing with Ted. "Bobby, watch out when you fish with him. You won't even be able to get in the boat the right way—you're sure to do something wrong." (Of course, to Billy Goodman's eternal shame, he had done something quite egregious: On a very hot day in the Keys when Ted was supplying everything else—boat, rods, lures, and lunch, usually an apple—and Billy's one responsibility was to bring a thermos of ice-cold water, he had forgotten the water. That, given the brutal heat in the Keys, was not a misdemeanor, it was perilously close to a felony.)

One of the worst days of Bobby Doerr's life had been spent fishing with Ted in the Keys. It was in Islamorada in 1961 or '62, before the developers had found and overbuilt the area; it was still one of the great light-tackle fishing venues in America, especially good for tarpon and bonefish. Bobby had been scouting for the Red Sox, looking at a catcher named Carl Taylor, who lived in Key West. Taylor was the half brother of Boog Powell, the big, powerful first baseman of the Baltimore Orioles, and the price on Taylor was going to be around $50,000, a lot of money in those days. So the scouting process was serious business. Bobby was going to be in the Keys for a few days, and Ted invited him to come by and do a little fishing. The tarpon fishing, Ted told him, was very good just then.

Here it should be noted that Bobby Doerr is a first-rate fisherman, a man who takes the sport with appropriate serious-ness. Any man who built one of his two homes in the most remote part of Oregon because of the steelhead fishing and who went there regularly before there was even a road into the area is someone who has obviously made fishing a singular priority. By Doerr's own estimate, and he is an uncommonly modest man, he was not as good a fly fisherman as Ted—almost no one he ever knew was. "Ted was so big and powerful that he could always put the fly twenty feet farther on a cast than I could," Doerr recalled. But Doerr could obviously handle a fly rod with exceptional skill, and the best evidence of this was that Ted always looked forward to fishing with him.

On this day, they had risen in Ted's very comfortable home in Islamorada (spotless, everything perfectly cared for, and everything put away, as if to stand in direct contrast to the grim, messy home he had grown up in), and Ted had said that he would do the eggs if Bobby would do the grapefruit, and almost as an omen of what was to come that day, Bobby had done the grapefruit improperly. There, in the home of one of the last great perfectionists in America, he had carved the grapefruit wrong. He had made one great circular sweep with the special grapefruit knife, thus separating the fruit from the rind, but he had stopped there, and regrettably, he had *not cut the grapefruit into little sections!* Ted did not explode at Bobby, but he did say something sharp about it, and there was no doubt that Bobby had transgressed, that he had failed the grapefruit-cutting test, the first but by no means the last test of the morning.

Then they went to the dock for the boat that Ted used—a small flat boat, about 14 or 15 feet long, with as little draw as possible, because so much of the fishing in the Keys is sight fishing and you have to pole the boat in very shallow water. Bobby had had to borrow a pair of tennis shoes for the day, and he tracked some dirt onto the boat as they got in. Ted shouted at him, Goddamn it, why can't you wash your shoes down? It was not a good sign. Billy Goodman, it turned out, was a prophet.

To go after tarpon, they were using a new casting reel that Ted had been working on for Sears; he had been hired as a fishing expert and adviser for the company. As soon as they got out into the water there were very big tarpon all around them, rolling on the surface, some of them, it seemed, well over 100 pounds. Ted was poling the boat, and Bobby was fishing, standing on the seat, on top of a tackle box, which they were using for extra height in order to spot the fish better.

Earlier, before they went out, Ted had been pushing to use spinning reels, which were more modern and less likely to have snarls, but Bobby, somewhat of a traditionalist, suggested the new casting reel, the new one being a more modern version of the kind of reel used before spinning reels were invented. They soon spotted a very big fish, and Bobby had cast out to it, and as he did, he sensed that the line in his reel was for some reason too loose, even though he had checked it earlier. Line too loose in a reel was a genuine problem because it could easily snarl, creating a complicated knot inside the reel, thus stopping the line from feeding out when a big fish began its run. Bobby had tried to tighten the line, thought he had succeeded, and now made a perfect cast. The fish, a big tarpon, at least 80 pounds, maybe more, had hit the lure and had jumped twice and then gone down deep, part of its run, but there had been a backlash in the reel, the line had quickly knotted, and the fish had broken off. Ted had simply exploded, at Bobby, the line, the reel, and the fish.

Bobby, something of an expert on Ted's language, had never heard anything like it before. There was an explanation of course: Here was the perfect day, the perfect fish, and Ted was being the perfect host, not fishing himself and putting his best friend on to a giant fish; everything had been perfect, and yet failure had resulted. Ted hated failure—for complicated reasons it was more threatening to him than it was to most men. Days like this, fish that big and ready to hit readily—first cast—did not come that often; it was far too easy for something to go wrong. Thus, in his anger, he began shouting that Bobby with his goddamn reel had really screwed up. This was a violation of the cardinal rule of fishing: When two men are fishing together and one of them breaks off on a big fish, the presumption is that the man who loses the fish feels badly enough as it is, and does not need to be taken to the woodshed.

They did not see any more groups of tarpon rolling like

that, but they did spot individual tarpon, lying on top of the water motionless, looking at a distance like giant wooden logs. Soon they moved in on another fish, but the angle was bad, and Bobby cast poorly, missing the chance to lead the fish properly, and spooking it in the process. The tarpon raced off into other waters. This provoked more X-rated language from Ted, and Bobby had a sense by then that, surrounded by giant fish or not, this day was going to be a first-rate disaster, one that he would long regret, and that an even darker Ted Williams was now emerging from the spirit of the man he knew so well and loved so much.

Just then they spotted another huge tarpon lying in the water, but the problem with this fish was that, given the angle of the sun, it was impossible to tell which end was the head and which the tail, a critical factor if you are trying to cast just above the head. So Bobby cast, and this cast, unlike the previous one, was perfect except for one thing: He had cast to the tail, which spooked the fish. At this point Ted was apoplectic. A brief, heavily expurgated summation of his tirade was that Bobby goddamn Doerr did not know a goddamn thing about fishing, that he had taken shots at three goddamn giant fish—goddamn trophy fish—and screwed each one up, spooking two, and breaking one off, though a child could have caught all three.

At that point Bobby's back began to hurt—he had a chronic bad back, which had ended his baseball career earlier than he had wanted. Standing on the tackle box seemed to be making it worse, so he stepped down, fervently hoping that they would not see another tarpon for the rest of the day. But then Ted started shouting for him to get the hell back up there, because there were going to be more goddamn fish. And regrettably there were. For right at that moment, they spotted the biggest tarpon of the morning. Perhaps 150 pounds. Just lying out there. Bobby's fatigue and dismay were replaced by the eternal optimism of all fishermen, that the last cast of the day will bring the biggest fish.

Bobby made a perfect cast, thanking the gods for that. As the lure moved near the tarpon's mouth, Ted said, "Give it a twitch," and Bobby did. The fish seemed to be eyeing the lure more closely. "Give it another twitch," Ted said, and Bobby did. The fish hit the lure hard, and took off. Then it jumped, majestic, bigger than they had thought, and then took off again. And then the line broke. Bobby was sure that he had done everything right, that the drag was set correctly on the reel so that the line was not too tight, and that he had handled the fish perfectly in their brief but exciting encounter, with a solid but nuanced tension point on the line. But the line had snapped anyway. What had happened, he decided later, was that the backlash on the first cast of the day had somehow weakened the line somewhere and created a stress point, causing it to snap later. Whatever happened, it occasioned the worst verbal assault on him yet.

It was an awful day. One of those days that stand out in a long and wonderful friendship for all the wrong reasons. Here they were, trying to do something that was supposed to give them both pleasure, but everything had gone wrong, and it had put their relationship to an acid test. Had Bobby Doerr been anyone else, someone not as balanced, someone not as comfortable with himself, someone who didn't understand Ted so well, it might have ended the friendship. But Bobby understood the complete context. That was Ted. They had been friends for some 25 years, and Ted loved him. What you had to do at moments like this was simply get through it and put it behind you.

What he also understood was that the person Ted was hardest on, excepting perhaps his wives and children, was himself. Up until then Bobby had thought there were two Ted Williamses: a sunny, joyous, generous one who could not wait for another day of life, especially if it involved a game of baseball or a fishing expedition; then there was the impatient and explosive Ted, unable to control his moods, as grown men were supposed to. For the first time, Doerr decided there might be even a third Ted Williams, someone even darker and more volatile, with even less self-control. They went to the house and that night Ted said, "I guess I was a little tough on you out there today." That, Bobby thought, was as close to an apology as one was ever going to get from Ted Williams.

Perhaps I should note here that I had a sixth sense about scenes like this taking place on the water, and though I am a very serious fisherman and get great pleasure from my time on the water, I had concealed the fact that I am a fisherman from Ted Williams when we met for the first time in 1988. There was a reason for this: I am skilled with old-fashioned casting reels and with spinning rigs, the chosen tackle for light saltwater fishing (bluefish and striped bass) off Nantucket, where I have a summer home. But I am not good with a fly rod, which surely would have been Ted's preferred instrument, especially if we had gone for bonefish, which I had pursued on earlier trips to Islamorada without much success. Fly-fishing demands a far greater level of skill than spin-casting. I came to it relatively late in life, and I do not get much chance to practice. I grade myself a C+ practitioner, although occasionally I fish for a week or so and get myself up to B−, but then inevitably I slip back.

I was interviewing Ted for *Summer of '49*, and I knew if I told Ted I fished, he would insist we go fishing first (his terrain and area of expertise) and do the interview second (my terrain and area of expertise). Somehow I envisioned pure disaster ahead. Though I did not yet know the story of Bobby Doerr and the giant tarpon, I could imagine one just like it, with me fishing like a donkey. Then he would no longer take me seriously as a reporter and historian. My grade as writer would be the same C+ I got as a fly fisherman, or perhaps it would be even worse, for I might unravel under the pressure of his cold and unsparing eye. Perhaps the interview would be cancelled entirely. It was all too great a risk to take. And so I was secretive about it and waited until the very end of our long day together, and then as we were parting, I slyly mentioned that I was a fisherman. Well, goddamn why hadn't I told him, he exploded. We could have spent the day fishing, and done the interview the following day. Yes, I said, it was a shame we had not gotten our priorities right, but maybe next time. . .

My day with him was magical. Because Ted Williams had remained properly wary of all reporters, the people he called the "Knights of the Keyboard," the visit had been midwifed by our mutual friend, Bobby Knight, then the basketball coach at Indiana. (I was probably Knight's most unlikely friend, as he was mine, but he had a fascination with the military and with Vietnam and I had one with college basketball.) The fact that Bobby had vouched for me got me over the moat, and so it was that one morning I was ready at eight A.M. at an Islamorada motel as ordered, when Ted came by, exactly on time, banged on the door, took one look at me, and shouted, "Well, you look just like your goddamn picture—let's go."

I got the first Ted Williams, as Bobby Doerr would see it. What I remember most clearly was the joyousness and the zest for life. There was a great deal of talk about hitting, much of it about his failure to get that goddamn Bobby Doerr to swing slightly up. For a brief time, Ted even worked on my swing—he was kind enough to say that he saw some promise in it. I am 6 foot 3, and I swing lefty, but I think that pretty much took care of any similarities between Ted and me. Ted also, I should point out, wanted to talk politics, and he was considerably more conservative and more hawkish than I (he seemed to have far greater belief in the effectiveness of airpower used in underdeveloped countries than I did). And since in those days the great issue of American foreign policy was the degree of intervention in places like Salvador and Nicaragua, he wanted to argue, which he did, in favor of going there and wiping out anyone who was in our way, and he brushed aside my arguments that neither of these countries posed very much of a threat to the security of the United States of America. I am sure that he won these arguments, because he had, after all, never lost one before.

I have spent no small amount of time in retrospect trying to figure out why it was so glorious a day. Part of it was the match-up—here I was at 54 dealing with a great figure of my childhood, in a scenario that allowed, indeed encouraged, us both to be young again, me to be 12, and him to be 28; part of it was a sense that he was special as a man and that he was, like it or not, a genuine part of American history (something I suspect that he had come to believe in some visceral way himself, but did not know exactly how to articulate); part of it was that he had lived his life in an uncommonly independent way, to his own norms and beliefs, and not those of others; part of it was the fact that at 70 he was still one of the best-looking men in America; but most of it, I decided later, was that he gave so much. It was the unique quality of the energy level—I have rarely seen it matched. He gave more than he took. In the age of cool, he was the least cool of heroes. Rather he was a big kid who had never aged and had no intention of aging; I was alternately dazzled, and then almost exhausted by his energy and his gift for life.

I have this view of him now, and it was beginning to form back then, that it had all come around to him because he was not a modern man, had always gone his own way, always outside the bounds of contemporary society, and had been so absolutely true to himself. He did not wear ties to tie-certified events. He had crash-landed his plane in Korea once because he thought that there was a better chance to preserve his body that way than if he parachuted out, which might have been harder on his legs. It was a bet, and he had won. He always, if you think about it, bet on himself. He did not go around doing things that would make him popular; instead, even when there were things about him that were appealing, he tended to keep them to himself. He was always his own man.

I think in that sense the .406 is special and defining, not that he was the last man to accomplish it, but much more important was the way he did it. On the last day of the season, Boston faced the Philadelphia Athletics in a doubleheader and Ted's average rounded out to .400 and Joe Cronin had offered him the day off. But Ted Williams did not round things out, and he had played, gotten six hits, and taken the average up to .406. Somehow that stands in contrast to so much in today's world where there is so much hype, and where too many athletes who

are more than a little artificial have too many publicity repre-
sentatives and agents, all of whom, it strikes me, would have told
their client to sit it out, rather than risk losing millions in en-
dorsements (and in all too many cases the client would have
listened). Instead, he had just gone out and done it, long before
the Nike people figured that slogan out, that they could make
lots of money selling the idea of doing it to millions of Americans who did not just do it. There was an alabaster quality to the
decision, and would have been, I think, even if he had gone hit-
less. The idea of Ted Williams choosing anything else seems
inconceivable.

Our time together in Islamorada started auspiciously. In
August 1946, when I was 12, and the Red Sox were making
their extraordinary run to the pennant, I had seen Ted play; it
was a moment when they were all still young and seemingly
immortal, and they had all returned from the war to find that
their skills had not deserted them. That summer, we were still
living in Winsted, Connecticut, where we had lived during
World War Two, and my father was finally back from the war,
and it was a big event for us, driving down to the Stadium, in
celebration of my brother's fourteenth birthday. Ted had hit two
home runs that day, as had a Yankee catcher named Aaron
Robinson, soon to be traded to the White Sox for Eddie Lopat.
One of Ted's two home runs had been the hardest ball I have
ever seen hit, both then and in the ensuing 56 years, an impe-
rial shot into the third deck in right that seemed to be rising

even as it smashed into the seats. And so we were sitting there, 42 years later in Islamorada, and I described that moment, and he had looked at me and smiled broadly, and said just two words, "Tiny Bonham," which was the name of the pitcher who had served up the ball. Later, it struck me that I had failed slightly as an interviewer by not asking what the count was and what kind of pitch Bonham had thrown. Surely he would have known the answer.

TED WILLIAMS AND BOBBY DOERR,
YANKEE STADIUM, 1949

FIVE

MONICA, BOBBY, AND DON DOERR, 1945

Bobby Doerr had deeply regretted that he could not make the trip with Dominic and John to see Ted one last time. He had made, to be sure, as many trips with Ted Williams as any person on the planet, starting in 1936 when Bobby was 18, in his third PCL season, and Ted was about to turn 18. Just out of Herbert Hoover High, Ted was so filled with nervous energy that he could never sit still. He was totally wired in those days, he always had to engage people around him in some form of debate or argument, he bit his fingernails to the quick, and he was bumptious without, of course, knowing he was bumptious, noisy without knowing he was noisy. What he did not know among many other things was that rookies, and especially skinny, teenage rookies, were hardly to be seen and certainly not to be heard, and he was the loudest rookie in history, and he became raw meat for the veterans, some of whom were genuine old-timers, men who in some cases had already been in the big leagues and were now working their way down rather than up the baseball ladder (which led to a *very* different and rather more jaundiced outlook on life).

Bobby remembered an early train trip when the veterans, who got the lower berths, decided that they had heard enough from this very loud kid, Williams, and armed with a few drinks they started baiting him, talking and talking, not letting him get to sleep. Finally, in desperation, Ted bundled himself up in his blankets and went into the women's rest room to hide out until the others had fallen asleep.

Then there was the train trip in 1938, the first time they went to spring training with the Boston club together. Ted was on a high the entire trip, more nervous and animated than usual, wanting to be the best ever, but, of course, scared to death that he wouldn't be. Babe Herman, an exceptional hitter, was on the train with them. He was just then coming to the end of a fine career, with a career batting average of .324, and Ted, of course, latched on to him. It was, Bobby thought, a match made in hitter heaven, because Ted wanted more than anything in the world to ask about hitting and Babe, more than anything else, wanted to talk about it. More, when Ted wasn't talking about hitting, he was practicing it. Bobby recalled wonderful glimpses of Ted on that train trip, early in the morning or late at night, standing in the car, working on his swing, using anything available for a bat—a sleeping car pillow, for instance.

The Williams language was already X-rated, and there was a group of older ladies in the railroad car with them, and they were not amused by Ted—neither by the sheer amount of noise emanating from him, nor its volume, nor his choice of words. They kept asking the conductor to keep him quiet, and it would work, but only momentarily. Soon Ted would slip back into his loud, uncensored talk. He never, Bobby decided later in life, changed very much in that sense. (There were a number of upper-class ladies in Boston, who more than 50 years later would vouch for that. For in the early '90s, Ted was having lunch with Tip O'Neill, the former Speaker of the House, when a similar scene took place. The two were having a joyous but noisy lunch in the dining room of the Ritz-Carlton Hotel, the most sedate of settings. Ted was a Republican, of course, and Tip a Democrat, but there was no more devoted Red Sox fan in the world than Tip O'Neill, which meant that partisan political divisions could easily be put aside. Ted was being Ted, which meant that the genteel ladies who made up the Ritz's lunchtime clientele could hear, whether they wanted to or not, almost everything Williams was saying. At one point Tip took up the subject of Ted's greatness, and in particular the additional records he might have broken had he not lost nearly five seasons to World War Two and Korea. Ted had long ago learned how to handle whatever disappointments, indeed bitterness, he felt about those lost years, and he realized that he had gained an extra measure of admiration for having served his country not once, but twice. So he fended off Tip's suggestions with great modesty: No, he felt no disappointment; he had had a great career; baseball had given him a hell of a goddamn lot; and he had gotten all he had wanted out of baseball, there was nothing he had been denied. *Nothing?* Tip pressed, *Nothing?* And so all the Ritz customers that day had heard Ted's booming answer: *Well, Tip, I'd have just loved to have had Larry Doby's cock,* a reference to the personal equipment of the first black man to play in the American League.)

That first trip in 1938 had ended with their arrival in Florida where Ted, meeting Joe Cronin for the first time, had greeted the manager by saying, "Hi, sport," leaving even Doerr, who had by then become one of the world's leading experts on Ted's brashness, sure that it guaranteed a trip to Minneapolis, the club's AA farm club, which it soon did. There was a certain cockiness to him that spring, a tendency to talk when he should have listened, and a comparable instinct to boast when he should have been modest—all a reflection of great insecurity—

that did not endear him to the veterans. In time, when he was sent off to Minnesota, a number of them were amused and let him know they were not terribly disappointed he had not made the big club. Off he went, more than a little wounded, vowing that he would soon return and make more money than any of them—which in time he did.

Back then Bobby Doerr was not just his closest friend—he was a kind of ambassador from Ted to the rest of the world, explaining him, pointing out that he meant no harm and that, yes, he really was likable, there was no meanness there, the noise was bluster more than anything else. That's what best friends were for, after all, and Doerr was perfectly cast for the role of young Ted Williams' best friend. Bobby understood better than anyone else his friend's passion to excel, his need to be the best, and how hollow his life was when he fell short of his own expectations. Doing well, of course, meant hitting. The rest of the game was somewhat incidental for Ted. No one loved his bats more, or took better care of them. No one worked harder on boning them to make them harder. Ted was the first of the power hitters, Bobby and others believed, to go for a lighter, whippier bat, to increase the torque, even though most of the other power hitters preferred heavier bats. He noticed everything about his bats, insisting for example that a bat picked up half an ounce of weight just lying on a field when there was dew on the grass. Others, lesser students of the game, disputed this. So, accompanied by some teammates, he walked over to the post office with some bats in order to prove his point. It was also

Ted, Bobby remembered, who first came up with the idea of using resin mixed with a little oil to give your hands a better grip on the bat.

Bobby remembered when Williams had made the big league club for the first time back in 1939 and they had stopped off in Louisville for an exhibition game with the Louisville Colonels. Louisville was where the Hillerich & Bradsby bat factory was located. Ted wanted to go there to pick out some choice wood for his bats. The two of them got to the factory so early that they had to sit outside on the steps for half an hour before it opened. In time, the top people at the factory came to know him well and to save choice pieces of wood, with extra knots in them, for him, and he in turn tipped them handsomely. That was Ted Williams when he was young and his career was just starting and in many ways it was also Ted at the end, though much mellowed. Bobby sometimes wondered what drove Ted on a day like that with the need to get to the factory so early. Was it a fear that some other hitter might get there earlier and get the better pieces of wood with the good knots in them?

Bobby understood from the very beginning that, no matter how much he loved Ted, he could never be like him. Bobby Doerr is very simply among the nicest and most balanced men I have ever met. I'm hardly alone in thinking that. When I was writing this book, I drove from my interview with Boo Ferriss in Cleveland, Mississippi, to New Orleans, where I spent part of the day with Mel Parnell, the talented Boston left-hander, who was then recovering from prostate cancer. Parnell and I spent a good deal of time talking about Bobby, and Mel said, "When I first went to the Red Sox, I met Bobby and he was already an established star. I was a kid, and I thought he was about the nicest teammate a person could ever have, and now more than fifty years later I've thought more, and I know more about the world, and I've decided he's just about the nicest person I've ever met."

That was not a minority opinion. Bobby Doerr was, there was no doubt, the most centered of men, straight and old-fashioned, a square, more it seemed to me, if we are using generalizations, Midwestern than Californian, less driven by ego than people from Los Angeles are supposed to be, which was not surprising because the Doerrs were German-American and originally from St. Louis. (Many of our clichés about ourselves turn out to be true.) He was always talented, and always good-looking—when he was younger, there was a kind of matinee-idol quality to his looks. Yet for all of that he was incorrgibly square. When he was a young wunderkind playing as a teenager in Los Angeles, he had not liked the young women who seemed to cluster around ballplayers. They seemed to him to be insincere and brittle, wearing too much makeup, with too much flash to them. Did they like you because of the kind of person you were, or because you were a star, a ballplayer? he wondered. It was not by surprise that he found the woman he loved on what was virtually the last frontier, teaching in a one-room schoolhouse in rural Oregon—sincerity of purpose was not an issue in the case of Monica. She could not have cared less about professional baseball or baseball stardom.

He was an all-American boy who had enjoyed an all-American childhood, and in time an all-American life, and was the better for it. Bobby greatly admired his father, Hal Doerr, because Hal had endured a very difficult childhood—Hal's own father ran off and left the family, and then came back and effectively kidnapped his own son. Hal, then only 11 or 12 years old, had been put to work cleaning stables and taking care of horses at the Santa Anita racetrack, and his father took from him what little money he made. This lasted for a year or so, until another family member spotted the boy at work and kidnapped him back. Unlike many men who experience cruelty when they are young and who become curiously desensitized to it, Hal consciously worked to make his own home a loving one, where no voice was ever raised in anger. Not surprisingly, the men who would later play with Bobby Doerr could never remember any burst of anger on Bobby's part, or him even raising his voice.

Hal loved the idea that his two sons played baseball. Hal had played a bit himself when he was younger, and he made sure that nothing stood in the way of his sons' baseball games—he was glad to cut the lawn or to do other chores so they could play. Bobby would practice endlessly as a boy; when he left the sandlot, he would go home to his room, where he would throw a ball against a pillow. His parents never complained about the thumping; once, when Bobby chipped some plaster, he was sure he was in real trouble—so much so that he tried to keep the chipped part covered up. In time, his father found the chipped plaster, but he in no way was bothered by it—that's what boys were supposed to do.

The Doerr home served as a sort of unofficial local youth center, especially during the Depression, when many of the neighborhood fathers were out of work. There was always extra food on the table, which made it a magnet for other boys Bobby's age whose fathers in those difficult years were less fortunate. It was not that Hal was rich; he worked for the phone company, first stringing lines, and then as a foreman. But during that grim era, the phone company cut back on everyone's hours, rather than lay men off. There was a lesson in that, Hal Doerr thought: The phone company, in both good times and bad, was steadfast and could be counted on by hardworking, god-fearing men to do the right thing. (Later, when Bobby began to make a little money, Hal told him to buy stock in the phone company, which he did, faithfully and conservatively for over half a century. Eventually, during a period of mergers and name changes, Bobby found himself owning stock in a company called Lucent. Deciding it was significantly overvalued he deftly got out just before the stock started skidding.)

It was all in all, Bobby later thought, close to an ideal childhood. He had all the things he needed, and lacked only the things he didn't. He was always very good as a baseball player, as close to a natural as one could imagine. "He looked," Boo Ferriss once said, "like he was born to play second base in the big leagues and nothing else. He was so smooth, it always looked so easy for him." In 1932, when Bobby was all of 14, he played for an uncommonly talented American Legion team, Leonard Wood Post 125. Doerr and three of his sandlot baseball pals showed up one day for the Legion tryouts and all of them made the team. In time, all four played professionally: Doerr with Boston; Mickey Owen (Cardinals, Dodgers, Cubs, and Braves); Steve Mesner (Cubs, Cards, and Reds); while the fourth, George McDonald, had a substantial career in the PCL.

In 1932, Doerr's Legion team played for the state championship in a best two-of-three series against a highly touted San Francisco team, which had Eddie Joost, eventually an All Star shortstop with the Philadelphia Athletics. The San Francisco players pulled off a great psychological coup before the first game, Doerr remembered: They took batting practice using juiced-up balls, and the balls just jumped off their bats, one hit after another going out of the park. It was a magnificent lesson in intimidation: "We watched them, and we were beaten before we went out on the field," Bobby recalled. San Francisco, he remembered, won the first game 16–2. But Bobby's team settled down the next day and won the first game of a doubleheader, 3–2, and the second, again 3–2. With the state championship theirs, they went to Ogden, Utah, for the regionals, and won again. Then they went on to Omaha for the Western championship—these milestones were noted in a series of postcards from 14-year-old Bobby to his parents. "It sure was pretty in Ogden. We got into Omaha about 8:05 Sunday. It isn't very

pretty here. I am okay. Hope everybody is okay. From Bob,"
read one. They beat Prescott, Arizona, in the first game of the
Western championship, but then lost to New Orleans.

Bobby played American Legion ball again in 1933 and
started the 1934 season with the same team, until he was signed
by the Hollywood Stars, who in time would become the San
Diego Padres. It was an article of faith in the Doerr home that
the children were going to do better than their parents, and
when Bobby started playing professional baseball, Hal extracted
a promise from him that he would return after the season and
get his high school diploma—which in time he did.

In 1934 Bobby hit .259 for the Stars. He was so green and
nervous, he remembered, that in one of his first at bats a curve
came at him and he bailed out of the batter's box. The old veteran catcher with the other team chided him, "Hey, keep your
ass in there, kid." He was lucky from the start, he later realized,
in that the manager Frank Shellenback was a kind, thoughtful
man who was very good with young players. Shellenback had
dealt with a huge amount of disappointment himself in baseball, but never took it out on others. He had been a spitball
pitcher for the White Sox in 1918, but was sent down to the
minors during the 1919 season. In 1920, while he was still in
the minors, the big leagues outlawed the spitter (although those
spitballers already in the majors were allowed to continue wet-
ting the balls down). That effectively ended Shellenback's
chances of returning to the major leagues. But he was a very
good manager for a kid breaking in, and he doubled as a

pitcher, still throwing the spitball, pulling down his cap twice when he was going to throw it. Sometimes a ball that he had slicked down was hit to second base, and when Doerr threw to first, he involuntarily used the slick part and threw a wild breaking ball to the first baseman.

Doerr grew increasingly confident in his rookie season and in 1935, his second season, he did even better, hitting .317. He had hit .360 for much of the season, but then slipped near the end. "Probably, though I did not realize it at the time, I was so young that my body simply wore down," he later recalled. What Doerr remembered about that year, as much as his own games, was watching the young Joe DiMaggio in his magnificent last season in the PCL, one in which he hit .398, but lost the batting title to a player named Oscar "Ox" Eckhardt, essentially a career minor leaguer, who hit .399 in 1935. That got Ox to Brooklyn the next year at the age of 35, where his 44 at bats made up the lion's share of his 52 total in the majors.

Every player in the PCL was in awe of DiMaggio. It was the kind of season that other ballplayers never forget, and some 50 years later Doerr found himself talking with Joe DiMaggio at a banquet in Toronto, and he asked him if that year had been his best ever. "No, not really," DiMaggio answered. "In 1939, when I was with the Yankees, I had a really great year. I was hitting .410 with a few weeks to play, and I got an eye infection in my left eye." That, as Doerr knew, was the critical eye for a right-handed hitter, key in sighting in on the pitcher. "The trouble was that McCarthy wouldn't take me out of the lineup.

And I just couldn't see as well. I went from around .410 to .381 in those last few weeks. I had to try and take a kind of side angle on the ball to see it better, but it didn't really work. I still don't understand McCarthy's thinking—I'll never know why he didn't take me out. I'm sure I would have hit .400. I had enough at bats, so it would have been my best season ever." (The Yankees won the pennant that year by 17 games over the Red Sox.) I asked my pal, demon researcher and Yankee season ticket holder Linda Drogin, to check out DiMaggio's story, and sure enough, on September 9, 1939, he got three hits to raise his batting average to .409; then he started slumping, and by our calculations went 17 of 73 for the rest of the season, which I make out to be a batting average of only .233. Thus, he ended the season with a mere .381.

In the winter of 1935–36, the Red Sox optioned Doerr, and he played one more season in the PCL. It was a year in which he led the league (and, in fact, all of organized baseball) in the number of total hits, 238, and also had the highest batting average of his professional career, .342. Late in the season, Eddie Collins came out to see him on what turned out to be a legendary scouting trip, one in which Collins effectively signed both Williams and Doerr. There had been a good deal of hoopla in advance of Collins' arrival: BOBBY DOERR CINCH TO IMPRESS COLLINS said one headline at the time. Perhaps there was too much hype. The Padres were playing the Portland Beavers in Portland, and Collins was in the stands. Doerr, normally the coolest of players, completely unraveled and made three errors, including dropping an easy double-play throw at second. Collins came to see him afterwards in the locker room and told him to take it a bit easier, and added quite casually that they were going to pick up his option. (Collins had already managed to see him and Williams play early on, nor was he the only big name who had scouted them—Doerr found out years later that Collins had asked Ty Cobb to keep an eye on them both. In fact, one of Doerr's most prized possessions was a letter to him from Cobb about bat weight and balance, which closed with a postscript saying how he had scouted Doerr and Williams several times at Collins' request. He had thought they both were sure things—in Doerr's case "a very fine second baseman and could not possibly miss." That was praise of the highest order.)

Off to the big leagues Doerr went; he was set to arrive in Boston just as he was celebrating his nineteenth birthday in April 1937. His first contract called for him to be paid $3,000 for his rookie season. When the contract arrived in the mail, Bobby had immediately protested by letter and asked for $5,000. In Boston, his letter set off alarms—this Doerr was supposed to be a good and modest kid, and here he was trying to rob the bank, even before his first base hit. A curt reply came from Joe Cronin, saying that Doerr's suggestion for his 1937 salary was "way out of line." "Bob," he continued, "your job right now is to establish yourself as a Big Leaguer." Well Doerr was young and green, but he was not that young and green. He and his father wrote back five days later, asking for the salary to be increased to $4,000, if Bobby was still with the club on June 15. To which the Red Sox answered that his salary would be $3,300, and that was the end of that.

It was on the same trip that Collins first saw Ted Williams. He loved the swing, just like everyone who knew baseball. He immediately tried to buy his contract from San Diego owner Bill Lane, but Lane held back—Williams was so green, absurdly young and skinny, just 17. He had been used sparingly that first season. Who knew how much a 17-year-old was worth? Collins said that was fair enough, he could understand that, but how about an agreement to let the Red Sox have the first shot at signing him. That sounded just fine, and they shook hands on it; the deal was essentially done—only the price needed to be fixed.

Then it almost fell through, Doerr recalled. Ted hit .291 with 23 home runs and 98 RBI in 1937, while Bobby was breaking in with Boston, and Lane's leverage increased accordingly. Other sharks were now circling in the water, but Collins did have that promise from Lane. It was Red Sox owner Tom Yawkey who almost blew it. That year's baseball winter meetings were held in December in Chicago, where Collins and Lane were supposed to meet and finalize the deal. But suddenly Yawkey balked. He had lately been paying a lot of money for aging stars like Jimmie Foxx and Lefty Grove, and it was all short-range, so they had decided to go another route: to build up their farm system. To Yawkey, who had had a number of drinks that day, the Williams deal suddenly seemed to smack of the old way (paying big money for a star), now officially known as the wrong way. For whatever reason—perhaps it was the cloud of alcohol—it was hard for the owner to understand that this was not the same kind of deal, that this was paying far less money, only $25,000 plus a couple prospects, for what was obviously an immensely talented kid. They were using the Padres as a de facto farm club, and Williams was not a player on his way down, but a wunderkind on his way up—a kid, with a stroke like Joe DiMaggio's. A deadline had been set for the Boston offer, as Bobby Doerr recalled the story, the clock was ticking, and finally Collins was able to persuade Yawkey that this case was different. Collins was properly terrified that he was going to miss Lane's deadline for a potential superstar, and he went tearing out of Yawkey's hotel room to meet Lane in his room. It turned out to be just in time—Lane was going out the door of his room on his way to meet with the Chicago Cubs to sell them Williams.

Because Bobby Doerr had arrived in Boston two years earlier, he knew the texture of the organization and he told Ted he was lucky to play for Joe Cronin. He was a man who understood the pressures on young players, and when he spotted tension in Doerr would always tell him, "Come on kid, relax. Sing a song out there. Let's have some fun." It was Cronin who tried to educate Doerr on how to deal with the premier threat to all American League hitters at the time: Bob Feller. The first time Doerr faced Feller, Cronin's advice was the essence of simplicity: "Bobby, just cut the plate in half. Forget the outside of the plate—you're not going to do anything against him with it. If he's out there, you're not going to be able to touch it. Or at least do anything good with it. And forget about looking for your pitch and looking for a strike. The ball will be on you too quick for that. You just have to go up there and swing on instinct." Doerr followed the advice, and did reasonably well against Feller, which was the great measure of success for an American League hitter in those days. (Joe DiMaggio hit eleven home runs off Feller, Ted hit ten, Doerr hit nine, and Tom Henrich, the Yankee rightfielder, hit eight.)

Success always came relatively easy for Bobby Doerr, and he handled it with grace and modesty. He never coveted anything that was not his. He was respectful of people who were different, and while he loved playing baseball and was pleased that he was rewarded so handsomely for it—if not in financial terms, at least in terms of admiration—he never let it distort his priorities. He always knew it was a game, and that there were limits to its social value. He knew there were many people who did other things, whose names were not known to the general public, but who were of far greater importance to the society than baseball players. He did not simply say this, he believed it as well, and it shaped the way he treated people.

If he had not felt that way, certainly Monica Terpin Doerr would have brought him back to earth. Monica had not, it should be noted, known easy times as a girl. Her parents were small-time ranchers in South Dakota, and she grew up on an

Indian Reservation before going to a regional teacher's college. Then the family moved out to Oregon, hoping for better times, and Monica ended up teaching in the Illahe area.

After that first fishing trip on which Bobby saw and fell in love with her, Monica thought he was a little slow in his pursuit of her. So, one night in 1937, his second year out there, there was a community dance on the other side of the Rogue River, given by the Civilian Conservation Corps (the CCC, which was a New Deal make-work organization for young men), and she made her move. It was freezing cold on the little boat which ferried them across the river, and there was ice on his seat, so she took off her black overcoat and laid it down so he could sit on something warm. "Why she lassoed me right then and there," Bobby later said, still surprised by what had happened. He, who had always been a little scared around girls, was at ease with her from the first. She was, in his words, "just the sort of wonderful person you always hope you'd meet." If she liked simple things and was comfortable teaching in a one-room schoolhouse, why that was not very different from what he liked. He liked small towns better than big cities and preferred the outdoors to urban life. He still liked to joke about the reason she had married him—that there were so few men up in that deserted region she had had no choice.

They were married in the fall of 1938, after his second season with the Red Sox. She had no earthly idea what baseball was about at first—she did not, he liked to say, know a baseball from a football when they first met. In time, though, she became quite knowledgeable about the game. But what he especially liked about her was that she knew so much more about so many other things—after all, she read so much more than he did. What he also valued in her was her flawless sense of values, and her ability to judge people—that is, who was real, and who was not. When, years later, Bart Giamatti, then on his way from being president of Yale to becoming president of the National League, told Doerr he admired him more than any other player in baseball and had a bad case of hero worship that had started 40 years before, during Giamatti's childhood in western Massachusetts, it was Monica Doerr who knew how to deal with it gracefully. Bobby had been surprised and awed that this accomplished, erudite man always sought him out at baseball gatherings and always wanted to talk to him at such great length. But when Bart Giamatti had told Bobby Doerr that he was his *hero*, that was a bit much for Moni. "Mr. Giamatti, you're the former president of Yale. You're a hero to people like us," she had said. It was something Bobby should have said himself, he decided, but had somehow not managed to say, and so when she had said it, Bobby Doerr knew exactly why he had married her and why their marriage had been so successful.

TED WILLIAMS, BOBBY DOERR, AND A NEIGHBOR IN FRONT OF
WILLIAMS' CHILDHOOD HOME, SAN DIEGO, CIRCA 1938–39

SIX

TED WILLIAMS, JOHN PESKY, AND DOMINIC DIMAGGIO

The idea of Ted Williams, frail, confined to a wheelchair, dying, was completely alien to his three old teammates. What they remembered about the man was his sheer animal energy, always just barely under the surface. When he was a young ballplayer he could hardly wait to get to the ballpark in the morning to take batting practice. What was it, Bobby had often wondered, that made him so nervous and impatient, so edgy in normal situations, and so cool in difficult, tense, or dangerous ones? Even when he was fishing, which probably relaxed him as much as anything, he had that uncontrollable drive, the need to be the best. When you fished with him you had to get out on the water early; if you dawdled and lost time, a huge fish that otherwise might have been caught might swim off to distant waters.

Bobby remembered scene after scene of that energy and that impatience. When they were with the Padres, there had been a scene at a local diner. Bobby was seated at a booth with some teammates when Ted came in, went to the counter, and slapped some money down—he was simply pulsating with energy, Bobby recalled—telling the poor, overworked waitress to hurry: He was in a great rush, there was a train to catch. He was in a rush, Doerr thought later, but not to catch a train. He was in a rush to be great. (One of their coaches, Doerr remembered, was a veteran named Eddie Mulligan, who had played in the big leagues with the Cubs, White Sox, and Pirates. Mulligan was greatly amused by Williams' frenetic manner, and would say of him, "What have we got here? We've got a young man who's in a great hurry to go nowhere.")

Ted was, the other three teammates decided, always a big kid. You had to accept him like that—with all the pluses and minuses that came with it. When he was generous there was no one more generous, and when he was petulant there was no one more petulant, and sometimes he was both within a few seconds. Once in the mid-1950s, Pedro Ramos, then a young pitcher with Washington, struck Ted out, which was a very big moment for Ramos. He rolled the ball into the dugout to save, and later, after the game, the Cuban right-hander ventured into the Boston dugout with the ball and asked Ted to sign it. Mel Parnell was watching and had expected an immediate explosion, Ted being asked to sign a ball he had struck out on, and he was not disappointed. Soon there was a rising bellow of blasphemy from Williams, and then he had looked over and seen Ramos, a kid of 20 or 21, terribly close to tears now. Suddenly Ted had softened and said, "Oh, all right, give me the goddamn ball," and had signed it. Then about two weeks later he had come up against Ramos again and hit a tremendous home run, and as he rounded first he had slowed down just a bit and yelled to Ramos, "I'll sign that son of a bitch too if you can ever find it."

To understand him, to get along with him and earn his trust, you had to take him on his terms. You couldn't change him. It was like trying to change a force of nature. You had to accommodate to him, because he could not accommodate to you. If that was something of a weakness when he was young, and surely it caused him on many occasions a good deal of pain and grief, then as he became older, as it became clear that he had never bent to fashion, it came to be seen as a sign of strength. Here was a man who had always been true to himself.

There were, in time, regular comparisons with John Wayne, suggestions that Ted was the real John Wayne, the last frontiersman, who lived outside the reach of the society's prissier laws. Ted, after all, had served in two wars, when Wayne, being of the right age to serve in World War Two but having children and therefore eligible for a deferment, had taken a bye to focus on his career, and served in it only cinematically. Ted was amused by such comparisons, the idea that he was more John Wayne than John Wayne. He would shrug them off: *Yeah, I know, but so what*, he would say.

Going his own way when he was young had not been easy. There were critics everywhere. He always fought back. He fought back when he was in the right, and he fought back when he was in the wrong, on the theory that he was never in the wrong. He did not know how to do the small, simple, political things that would have eased so many difficult situations with sportswriters and fans. Everything became an issue of personal honor and integrity. He was in those days—as Pesky often said of him, choosing a relatively mild word—cantankerous. The danger too, his friends knew, was in how quickly he could shift moods. One Ted Williams could turn into the other Ted Williams instantaneously and on the slightest of provocations. He was so easily wounded, yet he could also just as easily wound other people without realizing it.

Every slight seemed so permanent with him. There were too many incidents in which his distaste for the fans and for the press was expressed digitally or by spitting or by simply sulking.

He refused to tip his hat when he hit a home run and thousands were cheering, thousands who longed to cheer in perpetuity, but who, he suspected, had once somewhere back there booed him. Those boos were not to be forgotten, and he was not about to let them get aboard the bandwagon now, not old Teddy Ballgame. Opposing teams picked up on it immediately. He was too good and too determined a hitter to throw brush-back pitches at—he became even tougher when you did, and he always made you pay. But he had rabbit ears, which was the expression used in those days to mean he heard everything shouted at him from the dugout, and he treated them as if they were the verbal coin of the game. In that pre-politically correct age, much crueler things were said, and opposing teams knew they could always work on him from the bench, and they knew they could get to him.

It was as if he had to respond to every bad sentence written about him in the press and every boo shouted at him from the fans sitting along the left field line in Fenway Park. It was almost a compulsion then, the need to fight back. The Red Sox management did not help him very much when he was young; they offered no classes in anger management for raw, green athletes. There were older, wiser teammates, who told him to let it go, but he never seemed to hear them. If he did not fight back, he seemed to think, then somehow his critics' truths would beat his truths.

His one great truth was that he was going to be great, maybe the greatest hitter in the history of the game. And everyone had better understand that. He once got angry at Tex Hughson for failing a quiz on who was the better hitter, G. H. Ruth or T. S. Williams. There was one season when he got off to a slow start, and Bobby Doerr got off to a very good one, flirting in the early weeks with .400. Suddenly Bobby noticed that there was a cooling in their relationship, and gradually it dawned on him that he had violated his place in the pecking order, and by so doing had put a certain strain on their friendship. Any truths other than Ted's own—especially the ones written by sportswriters and voiced by his critics—seemed to him designed to prove that he was only what he had been when he was a boy: a scared, unwanted, unloved kid from a miserable home, that he could not redo his life to better specifications.

His secret truth was that he needed to be great in order to escape from that terrible home. He had been raised by an alcoholic father and a religiously strident mother who was out on the streets all hours for the Salvation Army. The phrase for her in today's vernacular would be that she was a woman in deep denial, very deep denial. She seemed to care more about the orphans of Tijuana than she did about her own two sons. Her home was a pigpen. When Eddie Collins had called at their home, Ted covered the best chair in the house with a towel so that Collins would not see the springs poking through a hole in the mohair. Ted was always fighting that shame about his background; when the Boston writers criticized him it was as if they were trying to make him once again the boy from that grim, sad home.

There was one aspect of Ted that few who knew him or wrote about him (including myself 14 years ago) understood, and that was his own attitude toward race and equality and how it was affected by his own ethnicity. If he was a conservative Republican politically, he was in terms of the workplace the most democratic and egalitarian of men, way ahead of his time in his sense of fairness. His acceptance speech at his 1966 induction into the Hall of Fame was memorable for his push to have Satchel Paige, Josh Gibson, and the other Negro League stars to be enshrined in Cooperstown, and for the way he had cheered on Willie Mays, then closing in on some of his records. Baseball, he had said, gives every American kid not just the chance to be as good as everyone else but to be *better* than everyone else. Other acts of kindness to young black players on other teams were remembered clearly by some of his team-mates. Back in the mid-1960s, Ted came upon a young pitcher from the A's, Johnny "Blue Moon" Odom, who was apparently having trouble getting a room at the hotel in Florida where his team was staying during spring training. Williams had under-stood immediately what was happening and why, and he had taken Odom under his wing. They had gone to the registration desk together and in time a room had been produced. For a long time such acts of kindness were seen as a reflection of the trauma, poverty, and dysfunction of his boyhood home. But late in his life it became clear that it may have been a little more complicated, that his mother, May Williams, was half Mexican (and half Basque) in an era when prejudices against Latinos in southern California were even stronger than they are today. The people who thought they knew him well had known nothing of this.

Certainly Bobby Doerr had never heard about the Hispanic side of Williams' family until very late in his life, when a little was written about it. And Doerr, more than almost anyone else, felt he understood Ted's shame from his childhood home. When they were with the Padres, Ted often went to Doerr's house for dinner when the team played in Los Angeles. "You don't know how lucky you are," Ted told Bobby again and again. "You just don't know how lucky you are. You've got the greatest parents. Your dad is always watching out for you." There was in Bobby Doerr's many scrapbooks (lovingly begun during Bobby's early years by his father) a June 1970 letter from Ted Williams on the occasion of Harold Doerr's death: "I can't tell you how badly I felt about your Dad's passing. The wonderful thing is he lived so long and died so peacefully. You were lucky to have such a Dad." The two young ballplayers had not, of course, gone to Ted's house in San Diego when they were playing for the Padres; it was just something that did not come up, and Bobby had a visceral sense that things were very bad at home. There were occasional passing references after daytime games from Ted that he guessed he would go home now and scramble some eggs for dinner, and Bobby had even then a sense of an empty, loveless place.

In the summer of 2002 I sat with Bob and Monica Doerr in the living room of their home in Junction City, Oregon, and I said, somewhat casually, to Bobby that I was sure that when they were young Ted had been drawn to him because Bobby was so centered and balanced. (Those qualities had sometimes irritated Ted as well—he sometimes got angry with Bobby for lacking, in his opinion, sufficient fire.) "You were all the things as a man he would have loved to have been, and knew he could never be," I suggested. By then Monica Doerr was badly weakened by two strokes and could not talk properly, but she readily understood everything we were saying, and would sometimes join the conversation, either nodding her head in assent or shaking it negatively. At this point she began to nod her head, but it was not the light nod she had used to agree with other issues, it was a violent nod, her head going up and down as if each nod were an exclamation point, confirming my point.

It was Bobby who had figured out over the years the extent of Ted's secret shame about his family, putting it together like the pieces of a jigsaw puzzle. He knew that one of the things that drained Ted was his brother, Danny, who was two years younger. Danny Williams was, as one friend who had known the family well recalled, nothing more than a punk, always stealing, always in and out of trouble, and, in time, in and out of jail. He was what Ted might have been had Ted not found baseball, and not been so brilliant at it, and not been so determined to lead a decent life. Danny had always been able to manipulate their mother's sense of guilt for not being there. When Ted began to do well and started sending money to her, she tried to use the money to take care of Danny's problems; then she would ask Ted for additional money, and for a time he would send it, but nothing good would ever come of it. If he bought his mother a new washing machine, then Danny would hock it. Ted, of course, quickly figured out what was happening, but he was unable to warn his mother off. "I could always tell when he got one of those letters from her," Bobby recalled. "We'd be in the locker room in Boston going through our mail, and he would get a letter from her, and he would hold it up, already wary, a little frown on his face, and then he would open it, and for sure it would be his mother asking for money. He was already taking good care of her, so he knew it was for his brother, and his face would darken, because she was willing to be taken again by her son and to use Ted in the process, and there would be a quick flash of real anger. And then he would take the letter and crumple it up and throw it in the trash basket. What drove Ted crazy was that he knew the money, despite what his mother was saying, was going to go to his brother, and it was a hopeless cause."

Doerr also remembered one particular afternoon when Williams' years and years of pain seemed to come to the surface: "I don't think I ever realized how deep the scar was until 1961, which was almost twenty-five years after we first met,"

Doerr said. "I knew there was a scar, but I just had never known how bad it was and how much pain it had caused. But then I was in San Diego doing some scouting, and Neil Mahoney [the head Red Sox scout] came through, and he had asked Ted to come there, and we were having lunch in downtown San Diego. And when lunch was over Ted turned to us and said he wanted to take us and show us his dad's photographic shop. And so we went across the street from the hotel, and there was a building there, all the offices empty now, nothing there but an empty building. Then he began talking about his father, who had not been successful, was out of work a lot, and had been drinking a lot. And as he talked you could just see it roll out, this little kid in this terrible world, all the unhappiness, all the things which had never gone away, and which had been stored up for so long. It was clear that his dad had never been there for him. And then when we came out he took us to this nearby corner, and he said, 'This is where my mother made me march with the Salvation Army, and I would try and hide behind the bass drum.' As he talked I could see it all, the little boy back then, the shame, and the pain and the broken home, and how much he had hated all of it. As we were walking around, and he was letting us into his childhood, I was thinking to myself, 'This is where it all started.' I'll never forget that day when he took us around because all you could feel was the sadness of it. The sadness of that little boy, and the sense that it had weighed on him so heavily for so long."

Ted Williams with a Louisville Slugger,
at the factory, 1950

SEVEN

DOMINIC DIMAGGIO DURING SPRING TRAINING, 1951

A s they headed south through Virginia, Dominic DiMaggio and Dick Flavin began to argue over what was the best way to drive. They were traveling on four- and even six-lane highways, and Flavin, being a somewhat conservative driver, thought they should stay in one lane as much as possible. But Dominic, clearly the superior geometrist-navigator, felt that if you could glide from the outer lane to the inner on curves, you would end up lessening the distance considerably. That seemed dubious to Flavin—at best on a trip of around 1,300 miles it might save a mile or two— but this was, Flavin realized, merely another sign that Dominic examined everything as scientifically as possible in order to figure out the right way to do things.

It was, Flavin was sure, the sign of a man who had been forced to study everything carefully when he was young in order to maximize his chances and athletic abilities. During his entire life, Dominic had fought all sorts of prejudices about his size, his eyesight, and his ethnicity. In the early part of his athletic career he had struggled for his rightful place, beating out men who were bigger and seemingly stronger, and who conformed more readily to the image of what a baseball player was supposed to look like. Nor had Dominic's business success come easily; there had even been a time back in 1977 when Jean Yawkey, Tom's widow, put the Red Sox up for sale, and Dominic had assembled a group to buy the team. His offer, he believed, was never taken seriously by Mrs. Yawkey, a theory confirmed when a local sportswriter covering the deal, who was a friend of DiMaggio's, stopped calling Dominic to check in long before she was supposed to make a decision. Dominic knew immediately that something was off, that it was not a fair and open contest to get the team, and he was quite wounded at the time.

Dominic had always succeeded by overcoming adversity. Nothing ever came easily for him. If Bobby Doerr had been the natural, playing with instinctive grace and fluidity, then Dom was the one of the four teammates who had struggled against the greatest odds. The scouts, the men who judged these things with their cold, analytical eyes, and who spent their daytime hours tracking high school and American Legion ball, spotting the talents of boys and trying to project them into the men they would one day become, loved a Bobby Doerr, and more often than not they barely saw a Dom DiMaggio in the beginning, or, perhaps more accurately, they stopped for a moment because of the name, saw the size, and then kept looking. He just did not look like a ballplayer. Somehow he always looked much younger than he was—as for instance in the photo on the cover of this book where even John Pesky, young and small himself, somehow manages to look older. Of Dominic, the sportswriter Fred Lieb had said that he looked like an assistant professor of biology.

But he had talent, passion, and purpose, and these qualities would more than make up for those things that most scouts did not see at first. He would become in time what John Pesky called "the almost perfect ballplayer: so smart and so talented. McCarthy loved him because he never made a mistake. He always did everything right. I will never understand why he is not in Cooperstown."

Dominic was the ninth child and fifth son of Giuseppe and Rosalie Mercurio DiMaggio. Theirs was a strong immigrant home, filled with the ambition to achieve more in this country than they might have in the old one. Giuseppe was a hardworking man who went out every day that the weather permitted on his fishing boat, and who believed in hard work virtually as an end in itself. Rosalie had been a schoolteacher in Sicily, and she always had a more expansive vision than her husband of what constituted a better life for their family. Hearing from relatives already in this country that this was a land with greater opportunity, she was the one who pushed for them to leave the small village outside of Palermo and to come to America. First they went to Martinez, a small town on the other side of the Bay, but she soon understood that San Francisco was better than Martinez, and so they moved there. Then she came to understand that they could find a better house than the one they lived in on Filbert Street and so they moved to Taylor Street, where the children grew up.

She was always more open to the new things in America than Giuseppe, even things she did not entirely understand herself. She knew that for her children to enjoy the full benefit of America she would have to take certain things outside her personal experience on faith. Not surprisingly, Giuseppe had an old-fashioned, old-world skepticism about anything as frivolous as American sports. When in 1932 Vince first played baseball professionally, he was regarded as the family renegade by Giuseppe, though this attitude softened when he understood that Vince was actually going to be paid for playing a game.

"You mean they pay you for doing this?" Dominic remembers his father saying with utter disbelief. Then in 1933 Joe followed Vince playing for the local Seals and he became an almost immediate sensation, hitting in 61 straight games—a PCL record. Joe was obviously supremely gifted at something that people in this new country took very, very seriously. Somehow that was a harbinger of great things to come, Giuseppe realized, and he began the process of adapting to this new idea of playing baseball as a job. As was true for many an immigrant family of that era, the Americanization process seemed to accelerate right in the middle of the birth order, with the younger children, especially the boys, allowed to do more Americanized things that the older children, especially the girls, were prohibited from doing because they were not the kind of things the family had done in the old world. (In some cases the way was easier precisely because the older siblings argued with their parents for greater freedoms for the younger ones.) For a time, Dominic, five years younger than Vince and three years younger than Joe, was assigned the job of reading and explaining the box scores to his father in the morning. Dominic knew the family had changed in some fundamental way when he was at Galileo High School and his father asked him one morning, "And when are you going to play baseball?"

A good question. Not that Dominic needed any encouragement. He had always hungered to play, to emulate his two gifted older brothers. He also understood early on that his size might work against him, and he would have to use his intelligence to overcome any disadvantage it presented. He had always been a good student, and was especially good at numbers. He never had to bring homework home; there was always a free homeroom period in the morning when he could get it done. When he graduated, there was a scholarship from Santa Clara, offered both for academics and baseball—even though Dom was hardly a superstar in high school baseball, batting ninth in the Galileo order, which befit his relatively small size, 5 foot 7 and 135 pounds.

College somehow seemed a bit of a slow track to him, so he went to work for a local box company. It was hard, boring work, from which he was rescued in time by an offer from a friend to play for the Presidio Army team, combining baseball with a supposed lifeguard job at $90 a month, a very good salary in the Depression. He stayed three months and felt he was getting better as a ballplayer. From there he took a job with the Simmons mattress company, putting springs in mattresses. But his mind was still on baseball; in 1937, when he was about to turn 20, he decided to give it one good shot. The Seals, in conjunction with the Cincinnati Reds, held an annual tryout for local boys, with the two clubs alternating each year as to which got the first pick. Dominic asked his parents' permission to attend—more because he felt it was the right thing to do than because he thought they might disapprove. By this time, their Americanization was significantly more advanced and they told him that whatever he wanted to do would have their support. Then he talked to his boss at the mattress company, explaining his ambitions and that in order to follow them he would have to give up his job. The boss responded quite generously, especially considering the hard times: If it didn't work out for Dom, his job would always be there.

The tryout was held early in 1937. There were, Dom could still recall even 65 years later, 143 boys who turned up, but he still felt optimistic about his chances. He weighed barely 140 pounds, and he was still an infielder then, but he had recently seen an eye doctor, who fitted him for glasses. That had made a huge difference. He could hardly believe how poor his sight had been in the past, how vulnerable he had been in this game where vision was so critically important. Prejudice against eyeglasses be damned—he had been batting in a kind of haze, and that was a high price to pay in order to look like all the other young men. He hit the ball well that day at the tryout, and he had a very good arm; he saw himself, because of his size, as a shortstop. But they did not make shatterproof glasses in those days, and the Seals, who, it turned out, were very interested in him, did not want him in the infield. It was much too dangerous; the ball might kick up off a bad bounce, break his glasses, and cause a serious injury. "With those glasses we better get him in the outfield," Charlie Graham, the team owner, said. By chance, they needed a centerfielder because they had just sold Joe Marty to the Chicago Cubs.

This was not merely Dominic's best shot, it was likely to be his only one, for he was a virtual greybeard at a tryout like this. But he had talent and the DiMaggio name certainly did not hurt—by then there was already some magic to it in San Francisco. In addition, there was his intensity. Nothing was wasted where he was concerned. He also got lucky in that Lefty O'Doul was both his manager and his hitting coach; O'Doul was, Dominic later decided, the best hitting coach he had ever seen. Lefty had already worked with Joe, getting him to pull the ball more, because he knew that in any number of big league parks, including Yankee Stadium, the left-centerfield fences fell away sharply. In Yankee Stadium it was known as Death Valley, and you could lose home runs there all too easily.

It did not take long for O'Doul, a man with a lifetime .349 batting average in the majors, to turn Dominic around as a hitter. Because he was so small Dominic had thought he needed to put all his weight into the ball when he swung. Thus, without realizing it, he tended to lunge at the ball. O'Doul quickly taught him that that was the wrong way to go, and probably saved his major league career in the process. By lunging, O'Doul explained, he was actually subtracting his weight from his swing, and thereby reducing its power. Many other managers would have looked at Dominic and settled for what he could do for them on defense in the outfield; they would not have cared whether or not he could hit and what that meant to his career. But O'Doul saw the passion and the hunger and was willing to invest his time in him.

What O'Doul taught him was that a hitter's power came from his legs, his hips, and his butt. What Dom was to do was wait on the pitch, keeping his body still, and then at the last split second start his swing, taking a very small step into it. O'Doul was very patient with him, and he would later tell others that Dominic was the ideal pupil, perhaps the easiest player to coach he had ever dealt with. "I'll do anything you want," the rookie told him, and whatever O'Doul suggested, Dominic worked on. What also helped was some early film of brother Joe, who by then was with the Yankees, his career soaring. He had come to a Seals workout and took batting practice with them, and a friend used an early movie camera to take some footage of him. And there it was on film, just as Lefty had said it should be: Joe poised at bat, head and body not moving at all until the final split second, when he began his swing; then every part of his body, in perfect coordination, seemed to lever the bat into the ball. Gradually Dominic began to adjust, to hold back and wait. It took about three weeks for him to get it. One of the hard parts was to keep his butt still, but Lefty was very good—he would stand near Dominic in the batting cage, and when Dominic moved his butt early, Lefty would jab at it with a fungo bat.

Dominic got it down one day early in the season in Coalinga, a small town in central California where the Seals were playing an exhibition game. It was a little town with a little ballfield, short fences, and everyone on the Seals was hitting the ball over the fence in practice. Lefty had asked Dominic to take batting practice with the regulars that day because he wanted to work with him a bit more. And suddenly Dominic too started hitting the ball over the fence. That of itself was not that impressive—everyone else was. But Dominic knew that he was hitting the ball much harder, that for the first time he was fusing all his strength into his swing, just as Lefty had ordered. He went over to O'Doul after practice and told him, "Lefty, I've got it now. I've finally got it."

At first he did not start for the Seals. There was a player named Brooks Holder, a good hitter with great speed. A converted second baseman, he had only one small flaw to his game—he could not catch the ball. The Seals pitchers tended to be somewhat underwhelmed by the idea of Brooks Holder in center, but no one said anything about it for a time. Dominic's big break came one day when they were going to play Sacramento. The starting pitcher was going to be Bill Shores, a knuckle baller. That meant a lot of balls were hit in the air, almost all of which Brooks Holder got to, but not all of which he caught. Before the game Shores went up to Lefty and said, "Skip, I think I can hold them down, but I don't want anyone dropping the ball on me. I want the kid in centerfield today." That was probably exactly what Lefty O'Doul had wanted, a pitcher to request the rookie, and he gave Dominic his first start. It was an auspicious debut: Dominic believed years later that he got four hits that day.

For a time he played only behind Billy Shores but then another veteran pitcher, Sam Gibson, who had been a starter for the Tigers and who had an underhand delivery—again, a lot of fly balls—asked O'Doul, "How come Shores gets the kid, and I can't get him?" "You want him," O'Doul said, "then you've got him." So pretty soon thereafter Brooks Holder went back to second base where he belonged, and Dominic DiMaggio became the regular centerfielder. It was the beginning of something important in his career: It did not matter what he looked like because the other players, particularly the pitchers, loved playing with him because he was so good and covered so much territory.

It took him time to get his hitting down that first year. For a while he hit erratically, and his batting average went up and down, but then late in the season he started to hit. On the last day of the season there was a doubleheader with Los Angeles and Dominic was hitting .297. He badly wanted to hit .300 because that was the magic line in baseball, especially for a player who wanted to make the majors; that was what the scouts paid attention to. In the first game Dominic got three hits, raising his average above .300. Lefty told him to take the second game off, but Dominic felt he had to do it the right way, particularly because there was a pitcher named Joe Berry who had been getting him out regularly, and he wanted one more shot at him. So he played the second game, got three more hits, and raised his batting average to .306. That he had played both games and gotten six hits was thrilling to him. Years later he would compare it, on a much smaller scale, to what Ted did when he got the .406.

The next year did not bring a great improvement: His batting average went up only one point. But then in 1939 it all came together for him. His body was filling out and he hit .360, losing the batting title by eight points, but being voted the most valuable player in the league. That year he was sold to the Red Sox for around $75,000 and the Seals also threw in a pitcher named Larry Powell, whose main claim to fame was that he had once struck out Joe Cronin, the Boston manager, three times in one game, giving Cronin an inflated view of Powell's skills.

Dom arrived in Boston in time for the 1940 season. By then Bobby Doerr was starting his fourth season and Ted his second. Dominic was quiet and reserved from the start—the immigrant's son sent all the way across the country to a strange city. The world of major league baseball was primarily white Scotch-Irish in those days, and more than a little rural, its humor harsh and raw, reflecting all too accurately the various prejudices of the era. It did not bother Dom at all: He did not push himself with his teammates; instead, he was observant, he studied the game, he studied what went on around the clubhouse, and he let people come to him when they were ready. He let his talent speak for him in the beginning—they wanted a great outfielder, well they had one now. If he did not pursue friendship at first, he remained true to himself. He seemed to know that if he did what he was supposed to do, played well, behaved like a gent, did not intrude on others, or presume with them, then friendship and admiration would come to him.

Because he seemed so reserved, almost shy at first, respect preceded intimacy. He also understood that it was a team in transition, that he and Ted and Bobby were the forerunners of a team which might emerge in time, a team that could win it all, perhaps year after year.

He went into the Navy after the 1942 season and was stationed in Norfolk, Virginia, as a chief petty officer. He played a lot of ball there, for they had a very good team, and in 1943 the Norfolk team arrived in Boston for an exhibition game against the wartime Red Sox. The price of admission, Dominic remembered, was the purchase of a war bond, and the game sold out. ("I think we beat them, too," recalled Dominic.) Afterwards Dominic was going out with his friend Jimmy Ferretti, who worked in clothing stores and was a real snappy dresser, as they used to say in those days. Ferretti dressed much like the movie actor Adolphe Menjou, Dominic recalled. Ferretti said they were going out to suburban Wellesley to visit his friend Albert Frederick. Emily Frederick, Albert's daughter, happened to be there that day, and the men all said hello before they went downstairs to shoot some pool. Afterwards, as he was leaving, Dominic stopped to talk with Emily, whose vitality quite stunned him. He remembered asking her what she did when she went out on a date but discovered she did not like the boy. "We go to the movies," she said. "Why?" Dominic asked. "So I won't have to talk to him," she answered. He thought her bright, funny, and easy to talk to.

He did not lightly forget her, though he did not write down the address, nor get her phone number, but four years later, during the 1947 season, his friend Ferretti had asked him for a signed baseball. "You wouldn't want it for Emily Frederick, would you?" Dominic asked. Well yes, as a matter of fact, he did. That was the way that Dominic found out that she was still single; he clearly was a man who did all things, including courtship, at his own pace. He had not written her because he was quite wary of putting his feelings down on paper. He had, it turned out, written to one previous girlfriend years earlier, a letter filled with gooey, sophomoric yearning, and the young lady who received it had apparently not been greatly moved, or at least not enough to answer it. So he became quite careful about any future displays of literary ardor. Now, Dominic told Ferretti that he would personally take care of this baseball mission—he would get some of his teammates to sign the ball, and he would deliver it himself.

He and a friend subsequently drove out to Wellesley. Emily turned out to be even prettier and more vivacious than he remembered. He recalled thinking, "She's not going to get away from me." The Fredericks were not, as might be imagined from the name, WASPS; they were primarily Italian-American, with a touch of German ancestry thrown in, and they had been in this country for several generations. Albert Frederick had done well in the paper business, in particular in the early recycling of paper. The Frederick house was filled with visitors that night, but Emily appeared a bit eager to escape them. She asked where Dom and his friend were going, which was out to dinner. Sensing that with this rather quiet, but attractive young man she had better take some of the initiative, she asked if she could come along. She had just broken up with her boyfriend. "I was twenty-four," Emily said years later, "already an old maid." They headed to The Meadows, a suburban dinner-dance club, where the singer and big-band leader Vaughn Monroe, in the midst of a run of very popular hits, held forth. In those years right after the war when dancing the fox-trot was still the hot thing to do, it was the in place to go.

She and Dominic went out on the dance floor together, and Vaughn Monroe, a man with a rich baritone voice, sang "Racing with the Moon," and then, spotting Dominic on the floor—Dominic was a local icon by then—he played "Take Me Out to the Ball Game." "Do they do that for you all the time?" Emily asked, and Dominic nodded his head yes, explaining that it happened fairly often. Emily, momentarily shy, said, "I'm not used to that kind of attention," and Dominic, using all the words he had saved up for the last three and a half years, answered, "Well, you better get used to it if you're going out with me."

It was an almost perfect date, although Dominic did say at one point as they were heading back to Wellesley that Emily seemed to talk a lot. But he was hardly the first to be so perspicacious. When he dropped her off, he later told their children,

Emily invited him in for some Lady Baltimore cake, a rather fancy dessert for him to eat so late at night; it was about the last thing in the world he wanted, but he thought she was special, somehow different and more alive than all the other young women he had been out with, and he knew if he was going to see her again he better go in and have the Lady Baltimore cake, and so he did.

She understood that he was reserved, but she did not think he was shy. Rather, he spoke carefully and thoughtfully, without any braggadocio. She knew that if she was going to see him again she would need to use a little more guile—she was not about to wait another three and a half years for his next call. So when they parted she took the baseball that he had used as a pretext for the visit and put it in the glove compartment of his car; that way he would have to come back to return the base-ball. And he did. It was a curious kind of flirting, a bit of Victo-rian England mixed in with a touch of Abner Doubleday.

Emily had actually seen him play once, even though she had absolutely no interest in baseball (a prejudice she managed to retain, though happily married to a famous ballplayer, for the next 55 years). She had gone to a Boston game with an earlier beau, a pleasant young man who had been to Dartmouth and who was a Latin and Greek teacher at a local school. He had seemed like the perfect date for her—after all she had been to Dana Hall, which was a very good school, and then spent some time at Emerson, which was also a good school. Her date had raved about the young player in centerfield and how good he was, but she, in truth, had paid no attention at all—neither to what her date was saying about the game nor to the center-fielder, whose name, now quite famous in America, meant nothing to her. The game had bored her. She could barely wait for it to be over so she could go to cocktails at a club and then have a nice dinner in town with the young man and his friends.

Her lack of interest in baseball did not bother Dominic at all. Nor was there any problem of ethnicity, as might have happened in an era when ethnic divisions were considered more important. Her grandmother, Carlotta, seemed to be rather proud of the fact that, though she was Italian, she was not Sicilian, and she had said something along that line one night at dinner, a snide zinger aimed at Sicilians, and Dominic had said, quite gently, "Carlotta, *I'm* Sicilian," and Carlotta, not one to back down, and not quite ready for political correctness either, looked at him and said, "Well, that's your problem."

Emily and Dom got married in 1948. She was hardly the prototypical baseball wife. She came to like some of the men who played it—Ted and Bobby and John were special, she always thought. She loved Ted's generosity, the fact that he was always there for her charity evenings, even late in his life when his health was failing and he was largely restricted to a wheel-chair. But the game itself, the thinness of the margins that separated success from failure, and joy from despair, largely escaped her. In 1949 after a tumultuous summer, the Red Sox arrived in New York to play the two final games of the season against the Yankees. Needing only one win for the pennant, they lost both games.

In the event that the Red Sox did not go to the World Series to play the Brooklyn Dodgers, Dominic and Emily had made plans to go to Grossinger's for a few days of vacation—Grossinger's then being a famed Catskill resort. It was something that Emily greatly fancied, perhaps even more than a few day trips to Brooklyn and Ebbets Field. That afternoon when Dominic returned in a grim mood to the Concourse Plaza Hotel, which was just up the street from the Stadium, Emily was completely oblivious. She was thrilled because they could now go to Grossinger's immediately. "Emily," Dominic said, struggling with the pain of the defeat, "don't you realize what's just happened?" It still had not really dawned on her, he thought. "Emily, we just lost the chance to go to the World Series," he said, and then added that they had better order up two cocktails from room service because he needed a drink.

Dominic DiMaggio

TED WILLIAMS, BOBBY DOERR, DOMINIC DIMAGGIO

EIGHT

TED WILLIAMS AND JOHN PESKY

T he Red Sox did not think of themselves as a star-crossed team during the war years. When DiMaggio, Doerr, Pesky, and Williams had gone into the service, all four were sure that their team was on the edge of becoming the dominant one in the American League. When they came back from the war, their skills returned as if they had never left the game—which was not true of a number of ballplayers— because a lot of service ball had been played against teams well stocked with other major leaguers. They sensed they were the team of the future—after all, with a median age of 28 for the starters, they were significantly younger than the Yankees. Joe DiMaggio was 31 in 1946, and there were signs that year that his skills might have been slipping and his once magnificent body was breaking down. Tommy Henrich, the immensely valuable New York rightfielder, was 33; Bill Dickey, the great catcher, 39; pitcher Red Ruffing was 42, and though he had won over 200 games for the Yankees, he won only 5 games in 1946; Spud Chandler, Pesky's quasi-nemesis, was 38 and having his last big season.

Surely other talented young Red Sox players would soon arrive. Best of all, they finally had a core of strong, young pitchers: Mickey Harris, a lefty, was 29 in 1946, and was 17–9 that year; Joe Dobson, also 29, won 13; and most important, two pitchers, just coming into their own, seemed likely to be dominant figures for years to come—Tex Hughson, who was 30 years old and had won 22 games back in 1942, before the war turned everything upside down; and Dave "Boo" Ferriss, all of 24 during the 1946 season. He had won 21 games in 1945, albeit against teams weakened by the wartime call-ups. No less an expert than Ted Williams, aware of how important it was to Boston's future that Ferriss' talents be real, was impatient to take batting practice against him during spring training in 1946.

Ferriss proceeded to move the ball around him very nicely, and when the batting practice was over, Boston reporters, seeking the answer to the same question Williams had been asking—Did Ferriss' 21 victories in 1945 mean anything?—flocked around Williams. He pronounced his judgment much as a venerable justice on the Supreme Court might hand down a precedent-making decision: Ferriss, Ted announced, had big league stuff. The 21 wins were not a fluke, and he would hold his own against the players now returning to the league.

Indeed he did, going 25–6 in 1946, his win-loss percentage leading the league. Hughson, unafraid to come inside and throwing a very hard ball that often dropped down on hitters, won 20. Harris won 17, and Dobson, 13. The four of them combined for 75 of their team's 104 victories. In addition, there was word in the clubhouse about a wonderful (and badly needed) young left-hander named Mel Parnell who had led the Eastern League in earned run average. Parnell was said to be a sure thing, and people in the organization believed he would add even more depth to the pitching staff. For once the gods seemed to be smiling on the Red Sox.

If anything the 1946 World Series seemed to confirm the promise that their future was unusually bright, and that they would play often in October. Their opponent was the St. Louis Cardinals, a tough, veteran team, that had ascended to excellence in the late 1930s and early '40s, finishing second in 1939, third in 1940, second in 1941, first in 1942, 1943, and 1944, and second in 1945. Much like the Yankees, the Cardinals' success was driven by an amazingly deep farm system. Branch Rickey, quite possibly the most skilled organizational man in baseball in that era, had run it with such cold, calculating efficiency that it was known as the Cardinal Chain Gang. The Cards always signed more desperately eager, talented players than they needed, paying them coolie wages, and often keeping them hidden deep in the farm system, which, given the labor laws that existed in baseball at the time, left the players powerless to escape. They were especially skilled at trades; when one of their stars showed the slightest bit of weakness, they would shrewdly trade him for a player from another team they had been watching for several years, often more carefully than the ownership of that team. It was a high-efficiency, low-cost system that greatly favored ownership at the expense of players. Not surprisingly, there were few weaknesses in the teams the Cardinals put on the field in those days: they had good pitching, their players fielded well, and they tended to run the bases well. The marvelous hitter Stan Musial was just coming into his own, and in addition they had Marty Marion, the gifted, long-legged shortstop, Terry Moore, the elegant centerfielder, Red Schoendienst, a future manager, just emerging as a deft, valuable second baseman, and the fierce Enos "Country" Slaughter, a man who seemed to play each day with a special fury.

Surprisingly, when the 1946 World Series started, the Red Sox were favored on the basis of the way they had overpowered their American League opposition; they had coasted to the pennant, with a record of 104–50, 12 games ahead of the

Tigers, and 17, yes, 17 games ahead of what seemed to be a stumbling, aging third place Yankee team. But because of the difference in hoopla, publicity, and scrutiny, any team which has never been in a World Series is never really favored over a team whose players have been there frequently in the past. But, it would turn out that, for all their greater experience in World Series play, in no way did the Cardinals dominate the Red Sox in 1946. The series was, in fact, as even as it could get, despite the fact that the Red Sox had to cope with an unexpected disadvantage as it started: Because the Cardinals and the Dodgers had ended in a tie at the end of the 154-game regular season, they played a two-of-three game playoff for the pennant. In order to keep the Red Sox players sharp and focused, Joe Cronin put together a team of American League stars for the Red Sox to play in practice games. In the first game, Mickey Haefner, the tough little Washington Senators left-hander, hit Williams on the elbow, and it immediately ballooned up. Williams went into the Series with an injury, though he never complained about it.

In the end the Series all came down to the seventh game, played in St. Louis at Sportsman's Park, on a field that was in the worst shape that any of the Boston players had ever seen. The game pitted Murry Dickson of the Cardinals against Boo Ferriss. In the fifth, the Cards scored two runs off Ferriss, taking a 3–1 lead. Cronin lifted him immediately, perhaps a little prematurely, Ferriss and some of the other Boston players thought. The score stayed the same into the eighth. In the top of the eighth, the first two Boston batters, both pinch hitters, Rip Russell and George "Catfish" Metkovich, got hits—Russell singled and Metkovich doubled to left, which meant there were men on second and third, with no one out. That was it for Dickson; St. Louis manager Eddie Dyer went to the bullpen and brought in Harry Brecheen, a lefty who had already won two of the Cards' three victories in the Series.

Brecheen had pitched nine full innings only two days earlier. A wiry, surprisingly slim man, he was nicknamed The Cat, because of the agile way he fielded. At an alleged 160 pounds—actually, some of the Boston players doubted that he weighed even 150—he was hardly a power pitcher, but he had a good curve and a devastating screwball, and so far he had been the Cardinal pitcher who had given the Boston hitters the greatest problems. That did not surprise some of the reporters who had covered the Cardinals that year; Howie Pollet might be the nominal ace of the staff with 21 wins, and Murry Dickson might be technically more talented, coming off a year when his record was 15–6, but Brecheen was considered a great money player, better in big games than in unimportant ones, and an unusually apt student of the game, which was critically important for a World Series where he would be facing a great many talented hitters for the first time. He knew exactly what he was doing with every pitch to every hitter, and he had sufficient control to maximize his leverage in most pitcher-hitter confrontations, rarely being forced to give the hitter the pitch he wanted. That year Bob Broeg, the young St. Louis sports-writer, had traveled with the Cards for the first time and done some embryonic pitch counts, and he found that Brecheen wasted very little energy and very few pitches—his counts were sometimes in the 80s for a complete game.

Brecheen, Broeg thought, knew the game exceptionally well and understood new trends in it before many of his team-mates did. A year later, Broeg had gone out to dinner with both Brecheen and Dickson, and he heard Brecheen caution Dick-son, who had a tendency to coast a bit, that the game was changing and that Dickson had better adjust. "Murry," he said, "times are changing. You can't do what you used to do any more—you've got to go out there and throw as hard as you can for as long as you can." The word used most often to describe Brecheen was crafty. He would eventually go on to become an important pitching coach with the Baltimore Orioles, playing a vital role in the development of their exceptional pitchers, and he was the kind of pitcher who often does well in a World Series against hitters from the other league who have not had a chance to measure him over a long season.

By the seventh game Brecheen had pitched two complete games against the Red Sox, shutting them out on four hits in Game Two, and then beating them 4–1 on a seven-hitter in Game Six. He had handled Williams surprisingly well, keeping him off balance, going against what Williams thought the pitch sequence would be, and always placing the ball extremely well.

He shut him down in four at bats in Game Two, and limited him to what Williams called "one chicken-shit single," in the sixth game.

Now at this most critical moment in the seventh game, Brecheen came in with men on second and third and no one out to face the top of the Boston batting order. That series was one of the relatively rare times that Dom DiMaggio did not lead off for Boston. Instead Wally Moses, a talented slap hitter, came over in mid-season, and was leading off, with Pesky batting second, and Dominic third. Brecheen struck out Moses, and then got Pesky to line out to Slaughter in short right field. That meant Dominic, who had knocked in the one Boston run earlier in the game, was up, with men still on second and third, and two out. He waited patiently at the plate as Eddie Dyer went out for the requisite conference at the mound to discuss how to pitch to Dom.

Even though he couldn't hear a word, Dom knew exactly how the conversation was going. With Ted waiting in the on-deck circle, they were not going to walk him, so sooner or later he was going to get a decent pitch to hit. The question was how they were going to pitch to him. Because Brecheen was a lefty and Ted was a lefty, and Brecheen had handled Ted with some success thus far, Dominic knew he was not going to get a very good pitch. Brecheen would be around the plate, but there was not going to be anything fat. Of Brecheen's pitches, the most effective was his screwball, the next was his curve, which he was having trouble getting over, and the least effective was his fastball. "If he hit you in the back with the fastball, you'd barely feel it," Dominic said years later. If there was an advantage that Brecheen had with hitters, it was that some of his pitches looked a little fatter than they actually were, and they enticed good hitters to try to do too much with them, to attempt to pull pitches they should go with and take to the opposite field.

The first pitch to Dominic was a fastball, which came in just a little high—Brecheen wasting a pitch and trying to get Dom to swing out of the strike zone. But Cal Hubbard, the home-plate umpire, a man whom Dominic greatly admired, called it a strike. "Cal," Dom protested, "it was high—it wasn't a strike." "Stop griping and get in there and hit," Hubbard replied. Good advice, Dom thought, just do your job. The next ball was a curve inside, ball one, the count now 1–1. Then Brecheen threw two screwballs in a row, both down and away. Dom bit on neither. That made the count 3–1.

Dominic looked down at third, where Joe Cronin was coaching. Cronin flashed him the hit sign. Dom quickly went through Brecheen's repertoire. He knew it wouldn't be that sorry fastball, a lefty throwing a very hittable fastball to a right-handed hitter, who was a good fastball hitter. That wasn't going to happen on 3–1. Maybe on 3–2, but not 3–1. It wasn't going to be a curve, because Brecheen had been having too much trouble getting that over. So it was going to be another screwball. But it was not going to be a screwball on the inside, Dom figured, because Brecheen would be afraid that he might jump on it and pull it. It would be a screwball on the outside. He was absolutely sure that was what Brecheen would throw. If he tried to pull it as Brecheen intended him to, it would more than likely result in Dom driving it into the ground. So Dominic decided he would simply go with the pitch.

Brecheen wound up and threw Dom a screwball on the outside of the plate, and Dom went with the pitch and drove it off the wall in right-center. Years later, Enos Slaughter, the Cardinal rightfielder, told Dominic that with two feet more, it would have carried out for a home run. Instead it was an extra-base hit, and both runners were going to score easily. Dominic went out of the batter's box hard; he was one of the fastest men on the Boston team, their best base stealer, and he knew he had a double, but he was thinking triple. If he got to third it would put even more pressure on Brecheen when he pitched to Ted, for he would have to be careful to avoid a wild pitch.

As Dom raced from first to second, pushing himself as hard as he could, he felt his leg give out. A hamstring popped. He hobbled in safely to second. The Red Sox called time and had a meeting at second. Dominic got up, but he could not run, and there was Joe Cronin, surprisingly tender, saying, "Dom, I'm afraid you've got to come out of the game." It was, Dom later decided, one of those moments when you were absolutely nailed by the fates. Here it was, by his own calculation, his best moment ever in baseball, his double had tied up the seventh game of the World Series in the late innings, and yet it was also his worst because he was coming off the field with an injury. He was replaced at second as a base runner by Leon Culberson.

Then Ted Williams popped up, and the inning was over. But the score was 3–3.

To no small degree, the game turned at that moment. Leon Culberson went out to centerfield to replace Dom DiMaggio, who was, along with his brother Joe, one of the two best defensive centerfielders in the American League. Culberson, by contrast, was a journeyman. His time in the majors was relatively brief—he made it to the big leagues in 1943 during the war, and when the war was over his career ended relatively quickly. Whatever else, he was no Dominic DiMaggio in the field. Dominic was arguably the most aggressive centerfielder of his era—he prided himself on the skill with which he positioned himself on certain hitters, he prided himself on the way he faced hitters, angling his body to the side, allowing him to get a better jump on the ball more often than not, and he prided himself as well on the way he almost recklessly charged balls hit to him, much the way infielders did. Certainly his brother Joe, with his long strides, might be able to cover more ground once a ball was in the air, but it was possible that Dominic got a better jump on the ball. The debate over which DiMaggio had the better arm raged between New York and Boston fans for years. Moreover, he not only knew the Cardinal hitters, because he always studied all the opposing hitters, but he had by this point, having done his own prolonged reconnaissance of the field itself, become as comfortable as any visiting outfielder was going to be with that dreadful, torn-up grass.

For the bottom of the eighth, Cronin went to a relief pitcher named Bob Klinger, a righty sinker ball pitcher. Enos Slaughter, perhaps the most driven member of the Cardinal team, led off and singled to center. Slaughter played the game unrelentingly hard, as if he were in some kind of war zone, often to the detriment of opposing teams, sometimes even to his own. He was in his prime that season, 30 years old, and 1946 was arguably his best season—he led the National League with 130 runs batted in. Eddie Dyer was partly responsible for Slaughter's unbending, uncompromising toughness, because Dyer had managed the 20-year-old Slaughter in 1936, when they both were with the Cardinal farm team in Columbus, Georgia, and Dyer decided that Slaughter had not hustled on a particular play. "Son, if you're tired, I'll get somebody else," Dyer said. From then on Slaughter always ran hard; he also changed, Dyer later said, from one of the quietest men in the game, to one of the noisiest. He was unusually combative and argued with just about everyone, not the least his manager and his teammates. Earlier in this series, there had been a play when Slaughter was held up at third when he thought he could have scored; he had bitched relentlessly to Dyer, until the manager, almost in desperation, finally gave him the right to go on his own, even if he did not get a green light at third. "You run, and I'll take the heat," Dyer told him. So the stage was set.

With Slaughter on first, Whitey Kurowski tried to lay down a bunt and move him to second, but popped up instead—a rare breakdown in fundamentals for St. Louis. Del Rice, the backup

Cardinal catcher, hit an easy fly to Williams in left, and there were two out, with Slaughter still on first. The next batter was Harry Walker. He was an exceptionally skilled hitter. Traded away to Philadelphia the following year, in the Cardinal tradition, for he was thought to have served his usefulness, he ended up leading the National League with a .363 average. In no way was he a power hitter (ten career home runs in 11 seasons), but no one in the league was better at making contact. He sometimes seemed not so much to swing the bat, as to use it to punch the ball, a move that appeared half swing and half superbunt. To this day, several of the Boston players can do an imitation of Harry Walker punching the ball, rather than swinging through at it—as if to show what a dinky, little swing it really was. But Walker was a very dangerous hitter in any situation, especially in this one. A great many of his hits, though he batted from the left side, went to left and left-centerfield. Dominic thought about that as he sat on the Boston bench. And there, as Klinger got ready to pitch, was Leon Culberson playing Walker like a dead-centerfield hitter. Dominic waved to Culberson, trying to get him to move toward left-center. Culberson moved a few feet, but in Dominic's opinion, not nearly enough. So he kept waving for him to move farther left.

The images that we have and which endure for most baseball players are those fashioned by a cumulative process, because our attention is so fragmented during the regular season—it is of uncommon deeds, great towering drives, or wonderful catches fashioned again and again by a given player reflecting both excellence, and *consistency*, until there is a certain permanence to the lasting image. It is based in no small part on the expectation that this particular player, a Mantle, a Mays, a Bench, an Aaron, is that much above the norm and will perform again and again to a higher level, and do the things he has so often done during the season. But the World Series is different. Because the entire nation focuses its attention so intensively, it is the venue where one play in one game, and one play by a player often otherwise uncelebrated, so holds our collective attention that it has its own permanence, and it becomes the defining image of the player. So it was with the next play, where it was decided for years that Johnny Pesky had somehow held the ball, while Country Slaughter raced from first to home on what was often described as a single.

The challenge to that account comes not from Pesky, but from his teammates: Pesky long ago accepted the idea that there had to be a goat, and that the honor, however dubious, was his. He had been raised within the codes of the game not to duck the role that the fates have carved out. But his teammates, most particularly Dominic DiMaggio, who had somewhat prophetically envisioned what was going to happen even before it happened on that play, and Bobby Doerr, think it is an unusually cruel and inaccurate account. They believe what happened was completely different from the widely accepted account, and that Pesky's willingness to accept blame reflected a remarkable stoicism on his part, plus an old-fashioned belief that to say anything else would be to point a finger at a teammate—in this case Leon Culberson. That was something that you did not do according to the codes of the game. And so it long remained Pesky's play. "Leon has been dead a few years now [actually thirteen], so maybe it's time to talk," Dom DiMaggio said in discussing it with me.

Dominic, watching on the bench and failing to move Culberson farther left with his hand signals, saw it all happen as if in slow motion. On the mound, Klinger did not try to hold Slaughter, so he broke for second and seemed to have the base stolen easily. At the plate Harry Walker, as Dom feared, hit a soft drive to left-center. Pesky had broken to cover second when Slaughter went for the steal. As he was going into second, Slaughter had a good view of the ball. (Walker later described the hit as a "dying seagull.") It fell between Culberson and Williams, and Slaughter kept running hard. Culberson chased the ball down in the outfield, while Pesky went to the outfield grass to take the relay. Meanwhile Slaughter, armed with Dyer's permission to go on instinct, continued to run hard. "I knew I was going to score before I hit second base," he later told Bob Broeg, "because I knew Culberson was in center, not Dom DiMaggio." The decision to go for it was a shrewd one, for aggressiveness tends to bring its own rewards in situations like this; if he failed, the Cards were the home team, and the game would go to the ninth and then perhaps to extra innings. So it was worth the risk. Because he intended to try for home, Slaughter had gone deep in the baseline on his run from second to third, so that he could hit third with full speed, not having to break because of the 90-degree corner. As he reached third, Mike Gonzales, the third base coach, tried to hold him up, but Slaughter ran right through the signal.

The noise in the ballpark was fearsome. The Cardinal fans, knowing Slaughter, knowing the way he played, sensed what was happening before the Red Sox players did, and they were cheering wildly. Those Boston players who did see what was happening were unable to alert their teammates in the din. In the outfield, Culberson was a little slow to retrieve the ball and when he did, he seemed oblivious to what was happening back in the infield. Probably his throw should have gone toward home, with a cut-off man taking it, but instead he threw to Pesky on the outfield grass. The throw to Pesky was soft—a lob, really, the other Boston players remembered—and Pesky took the ball with his back to the plate. He was blind on the play, unable to hear Bobby Doerr or anyone else trying to alert him. (Slaughter, years after all this happened, told the writer Tom Wicker that he saw Pesky catch the ball and turn momentarily towards second base; that account now seems unlikely to both Wicker and me as we reconstruct the play, given how hard Slaughter was running and the way he was closing in on third, ready to cut the base perfectly, as film clips show, and using his right, or outside, foot to hit the bag. It is hard to believe that Pesky was in his sight line by then.)

When Pesky got the ball he turned towards the infield, picked up Slaughter, and finally understood what was happening; it was probably already too late, for Slaughter was closing in on home. Some baseball people, including the eminent Boston sports historians Glen Stout and Richard Johnson, who have studied the film of that moment, much as anthropologists study rare new evidence of the eating habits of now exotic tribes, have detected—I looking at the same film am not able to—an element of surprise in Pesky's body language as he finally realizes what Slaughter is doing. In their extremely careful history of the team, *Red Sox Century*, they say that Pesky neither freezes nor pauses as he gets the ball, though because of the way he catches the ball, he has to go to "a quick half windup." Culberson's throw to Pesky had been a bad one, as Johnson and Stout and others (including Pesky) have noted; it came in around his waist, and Pesky had to raise the ball up, going to what was a partial windup before he threw home. He never really had a chance. His throw to the plate was offline, about eight or ten feet up the line towards third, and Slaughter scored virtually without a play at the plate.

In those days television did not cover the World Series—it started to the next year—and there was no marvelous instant replay to help figure out what had happened. Many radio and print reporters were fooled by the play; much like the Red Sox players, they had been behind in picking up what was happening on the field. They decided that Pesky had held the ball, which probably he did for a tiny fraction of a second, and he was named the goat of the Series. That became a surprisingly permanent image—for years, millions of baseball fans knew of John Pesky not because he had great bat control and had led the league for three years in hits, but because he allegedly had held the ball while Country Slaughter had dashed home. Indeed in the mythology of the play, Slaughter was often credited for going from first to home on a single, although Walker's hit was technically a double. (The decision by the three official scorers to call Walker's hit a double instead of a single so appalled Bob Broeg, then a young rookie sportswriter for the *St. Louis Post-Dispatch* covering his first World Series, that the moment the game was over he went over to the scorers, and told them, "Gentlemen, by scoring that as a double, you've taken the romance out of a great play.") After the game, Pesky spoke with reporters in the locker room, and he took all the blame. "If I was alert, I'd have had him," he said. "When I finally woke up and saw him running for home, I couldn't have gotten him with a .22."

Watching the play had been pure agony for Dominic DiMaggio because he had seen it all coming so clearly. Because Culberson was playing Walker wrong, the ball had gotten into the gap. Because the outfield was rough and bumpy, and Leon was unaccustomed to it and not very confident, Dominic believed, he had played the ball conservatively. His own injury, his own pulled hamstring, Dominic now decided, had become the decisive play of the game. He always wondered whether he would have been able to throw Slaughter out at *third* had he been playing. There would have been, he knew, no question of Slaughter going home—why, Slaughter told him that himself, years later. One of the cruelest things about the game and the play, Dominic thought, was that almost no one really understood what had happened, and Pesky had been forced to take all the heat.

Bobby Doerr agreed. "All these years later people are still talking about that play," Doerr said. "And they ask, 'Why didn't someone yell out to John?' Well I was there, and you couldn't hear a thing. They say John held the ball. He didn't. He was blind to what was happening, deaf to his teammates, and he made a normal play. Slaughter made a great play. If Dominic is out there in center, Slaughter stays on third base. Period." The thing that no one remembers, Doerr added, "is how terrible the field was. It was just brutal—as bad a field as I've ever played on. So bumpy and rough. Dom was accustomed to it by then, and not afraid of it. But Leon was very tentative with it. Dominic played balls aggressively; Leon played this one conservatively."

Fifty-six years after that play, Johnny Pesky is sitting in his home in Swampscott. "I can remember the play as clearly as ever," Pesky is telling me, "like it was yesterday. Going over to cover second when Slaughter originally broke, because Walker was left-handed. Then Walker hitting that soft fly to left center, the ball hanging up there so long, slowing the play down, helping Slaughter, the ball coming down in the gap. And then I was taking the throw from Leon." At this point he gets up and does an imitation of a soft lob coming in to him. "By the time I turned and picked up Slaughter, he was virtually home. They decided to make me the goat afterwards, and I decided I could take it—I could live with it. If they want to blame me, they can blame me. Because none of it changes what happened on the field. We lost. That's what happened on the field."

He never tried to exonerate himself or to explain the play. "You can't argue with people," he says, "about what they thought they saw even if they didn't see it." Over the years his teammates, especially Dom and Bobby, would try to explain to others what happened on the play, that John's role in it had been minimal, but Pesky himself never did. That was something he had learned hanging around the old Portland clubhouse. There were some old-timers there, including a veteran pitcher named Bill Posedel, a man who was 13 years older than John. He had warned John that the worst thing you could ever do in baseball was to try to shift the blame when others placed it on you. It didn't matter if the blame was being apportioned fairly or not; if you tried to run from what people believed, then you only made it worse, and dug yourself in deeper. But if you accepted it, then you ended up a better man, and your team-mates would know, and so would those few other people who needed to know. "Look, John," Posedel had said many times to Pesky in the clubhouse, "it's not a perfect game. Things go wrong. And when they go wrong, you can't fight it. It's easy to deal with things when they go right. It's dealing with them when they go wrong that determines whether you're a man or not. That's the way you become a man."

The play effectively ended the Series. The Red Sox put two men on in the ninth but failed to move them around properly. Ted Williams wept openly after the game. He had not had a good Series. The Cards had gone into a full shift on him, almost

daring him to try to hit to left, and Williams had refused the
dare. Whether because of his bad elbow or shrewd Cardinal
pitching he had only five hits and one RBI. (After the '46 All
Star game, Ty Cobb wrote Ted a letter telling him how to beat
the shift by going to left field, and Bobby Doerr was with Ted
when he opened the letter and read it. Hell, Ted had said, that's
not what I'm paid to do. Then he had torn up the letter. "Can
you imagine what that letter would be worth today in the
memorabilia business? Ty Cobb writing to Ted Williams on
how to beat the shift? One million? Two million?" Doerr
laughs, telling the story.)

The Red Sox's disappointment was muted by the belief
that surely this defeat was only temporary. They had run away
from the Yanks, they had played the veteran Cardinals virtually
dead even. They had a great core team, and their homegrown
pitchers had finally arrived. Bobby Doerr, who measured these
things very carefully, thought they were set for five or six
years—in all likelihood, that meant, for the remainder of their
careers. They liked each other and there was true joy, he believed, in playing with men whom you liked and whom you
trusted—especially when you had a great player like Ted, who
so rarely would go on a prolonged slump. There was a lot to be
optimistic about.

If there had been doubts about Boo Ferriss before the season started, his 25–6 record and the way he pitched in the
World Series ended them. He was a wonderful pitcher, Doerr
thought, with a first-rate sinker and a good curve. Everything

from him seemed to drop down. It was hard to think of a young pitcher in the American League who had a brighter future. Tex Hughson was just as tough. He had a sinking fastball; he seemed to delight in coming inside with his meanest pitches. As such he was the type of pitcher whom hitters hated to bat against. Bobby thought the two of them could each be counted on for 20–25 wins a year for several years. And there was talk of Mel Parnell, the young left-hander who everyone said had big league stuff. The future seemed to be set, and it seemed to be theirs.

In 1947, though, both Ferriss and Hughson came up with arm problems, and neither was ever the same. Mickey Harris, only 30, came up with a bad arm as well and seemed to age overnight. With that went the dream. Instead of having the best pitching staff in the American League, the Red Sox had to start almost from scratch, even as the Yankees put together two trades for pitchers—Joe Gordon for the hard-throwing righty Allie Reynolds, and Aaron Robinson for the shrewd junk baller Eddie Lopat. Suddenly the Yankees had a wondrous pitching staff led by Reynolds, Lopat, and Vic Raschi, and in 1950 they added Whitey Ford.

More than 50 years later, Bobby Doerr still wondered what had happened to Ferriss and Hughson and, more importantly, why it happened. One day the future seemed to be theirs, and the next day everything was cut out from under them. What had gone wrong? Why had it gone wrong? Were the Red Sox dogged by dark fortune? Were they star-crossed or were they, in the lexicon of sports, snake-bit?

It all ended up being so personal, Doerr thought. His hopes and those of the others were inextricably bound up in what happened to Ferriss and Hughson. Had Cronin, a player's manager, overused them in 1946 and asked them to pitch too many innings? Did both of them try and come back too soon from their arm injuries? If things had gone right, Doerr thought, they might have won three pennants in a row: in 1948, when they tied at the end of the regular season with Cleveland and then lost a winner-take-all playoff to the Indians, after Joe McCarthy stunned even his own players and started Denny Galehouse instead of a rested Mel Parnell in the game; in 1949 when they lost to the Yankees on the final day of the season, carried all season by only two pitchers, Parnell and Ellis Kinder, who served as the team's best relievers as well as prime starters, the two appearing in a total of 82 of Boston's 154 games; and in 1950, when they finished 4 games behind the Yankees: By that point Hughson was gone from the game completely and Boo Ferriss pitched only one inning of one game. Even if each had won only 15 games, Doerr thought, it would have been more than enough for three additional pennants.

The night Bobby Doerr and I talked about what had happened to Ferriss and Hughson, we were having dinner at a restaurant halfway between Junction City and Eugene, Oregon, where Don Doerr (Bob and Monica's son), who is retired after a career as an accountant, lives. Don asked his father if they did pitch counts in those days. No, Bobby answered, pitch counts were far, far in the future. In those days, a pitcher started a game and he was expected to pitch nine innings each time he went out. It was almost a manhood thing. That was a lot of innings, and in those days they had nothing like the medical procedures they have today for arm problems. With both Ferriss and Hughson bedeviled by sore arms, any hopes of a dynasty had died.

Tex Hughson died in 1993, but 14 years ago I visited him in San Marcos, Texas, where he had done well in real estate as the town had expanded. He told me in excruciating detail of the pain he had suffered the year his arm went dead, and he explained why he had never been the same pitcher: It was a fluke, he said, an injury not unlike that suffered later on by both Whitey Ford and J. R. Richard of Houston—an overdeveloped muscle cutting off the circulation in his pitching arm.

Now, still seeking the answers to Bobby Doerr's questions, I went looking for Boo Ferriss, who, at the age of 81, is retired from his job as the baseball coach of Delta State University in Cleveland, Mississippi. I had interviewed him once before, for *Summer of '49*, but didn't know how to reach him currently. The Red Sox office gave me a number, but when I dialed it, I was told that what I had was not a working number. So I called information and asked for Dave Ferriss and was given a different number. A relatively young voice answered the phone.

"I'm looking for Dave Ferriss," I said. "This is Dave Ferriss," came the reply. "Dave Ferriss, the old Boston Red Sox pitcher?" I asked with some measure of disbelief. "I have a feeling you want my grandfather," the voice said. He gave me his grandfather's phone number, and I called him. "Well, I'm not in the phone book as Dave," the old pitcher said. "I'm in it as Boo Ferriss. That's what everyone down here calls me."

Ferriss is a legend in the Mississippi Delta, a country boy from Shaw, Mississippi, whose father was a small-time cotton farmer and whose mother worked in the local post office. Boo pitched for Boston in the World Series at the age of 24. The last time I interviewed him, in 1988, my beloved friend Willie Morris, the wonderful Mississippi writer who once had been my boss at *Harper's* magazine, came with me. Boo was a big hero to Willie, who loved baseball, and Willie always remembered that when Boo pitched in the World Series he and the other kids in Yazoo City—Willie was, I believe, in the seventh grade that year—were given part of the day off so they could go home and listen on the radio because a Mississippi boy was about to do them proud in the World Series.

Willie had driven me to Boo's house and had sat with me throughout—the rare instance when I let anyone sit in on one of my interviews, but it was pure baseball heaven for Willie, who kept nodding in agreement whenever Boo said something. It was as if Boo was talking not just about his own boyhood and his years with Boston, but *Willie's* boyhood and *his* years with the Red Sox as well, and it was Willie, as well as Boo, who had pitched in that World Series. I thought about that day when almost a decade later, in August 1999, I went to Mississippi for Willie's funeral. Because he was something of a Mississippi legend his body had rested in the Old Capitol and thousands had come by to pay their respects. Boo, it turned out, had been very much aware of his fame when we first visited him, that he had something of a regional laureate with him that day. "He sat right here, and you sat right there in the same chair you're in now," he said pointing at two chairs in his living room. "I tell folks it was very literary here that day in the Ferriss home. We don't get a lot of writers here—we were surely honored that day."

Boo Ferriss was a smart pitcher; he knew exactly what he could do and what he could not. "I wasn't a power pitcher, and I didn't throw in the nineties like most of them today. My breaking ball was a curve, and my best pitch was the sinker that bore in on right-handed hitters, and away from lefties. For me to be successful, my control had to be very good. I wasn't going to strike out a lot of hitters. If I got four or five strikeouts a game that was a good game," he said. "Tex was stronger than I was, and he threw a heavy ball." Boo managed to remain close to his teammates over the years, which was difficult, not just because his career was relatively brief, but also because pitchers and position players are rarely that close. In fact, they are natural adversaries of sorts, even when they are on the same team. That became clear to Boo some 20 years ago when Ted Williams flew down to Mississippi to make an appearance for Sears and came by the ballpark that Boo had lovingly constructed for his Delta

State team. It was a handsome ballpark for a small college, but Ted immediately seized on the crucial missing ingredient. "Just like a blankety-blank pitcher," he said. (Boo Ferriss does not curse.) "There's no background wall for the hitters." The next year Ferriss got enough additional money to build the wall, and he called Ted to tell him it had been done. "Well, okay," Williams had said, "but just remember you're a little late."

Ferriss hurt his arm one day in Cleveland during the 1947 season. He broke off a curve, a good curve, and then the next day he couldn't feel anything in his arm. It was what would eventually be called a rotator cuff injury, Boo is now certain, and although there is restorative surgery for it now, there was none then. He and Bobby Doerr have remained good friends over the years, and they have talked often about what happened to his arm back then. They both now believe that he probably pitched too many innings—265 in 1945, 274 in 1946, and before that at least 200 playing with a service team back at Randolph Field. "When I talk to Bobby, and we look back at what happened, I don't think there's any doubt that I was pitching too much, and that my arm was really tired. Tex and I pitched every three days back then. One year the four of us won seventy-five games, and we had so much to look forward to, and then it was mostly gone."

Such for the dynasty. The great pitching staff never materialized. In 1948 Mel Parnell came up and proved to be even better than anyone expected, and the Red Sox got lucky in a couple of trades with the hapless St. Louis Browns in which 12 players and $375,000 changed hands, getting Vern Stephens and Jack Kramer one day and the next, in what was essentially part of the previous day's deal, getting an older pitcher named Ellis Kinder. Kinder turned out to be a great success, a shrewd country boy who had made it to the big leagues just as he was turning 32. It was one of the last deals done primarily with Yawkey's money, and it bought the Red Sox a little time. But the Yankees—with Vic Raschi, Allie Reynolds, Eddie Lopat, and then Whitey Ford—were deeper in pitching and deeper in their farm system, always able to find the one player they needed. As a result they dominated the 1950s.

There was a fairly simple formula to New York's success: good pitching, good defense, and then just enough hitting to win, Doerr thought. It was as if the Yankee farm system was premised on producing good pitchers, good, steady middle-infielders, and one great All Star quality catcher—Doerr believed the great catcher was critical. Dominic agreed with that. When he was in the Navy, Dom had written to Joe Cronin, warning him that the Yankees had a good young catcher coming up through their system. "I told our people that if they thought their problems were going to be over because Bill Dickey was near retirement they better think again because the Yankees had a kid in Norfolk and he could throw and hit and he was going to be good, this kid Berra. He had some problems with foul balls, but I knew they could work with him on that, and that we were in trouble behind the plate—it was always one of their strengths and one of our weaknesses."

They all had regrets about those lost pennants. Almost 40 years after they had lost out on the last day of the 1949 season, Ted Williams would sit in his home in Florida and talk to me about the dying quail blooper that Jerry Coleman of the Yankees hit to win that game, a victory that gave the Yankees the pennant. "Oh God," Ted told me that day, "that cheap hit, that cheap goddamn hit. Coleman is up. Tex makes a good pitch. A damn good pitch. Then Bobby is going back and Zeke [Al Zarilla] is coming in. Oh Jesus, I can still see it with my eyes closed. Zeke is diving for it, and then I can see it squirting to the foul line. It's funny how you can remember something so painful so clearly. God, the locker room was silent. Like we were all dead. McCarthy was graceful. He had to be in terrible pain, but he went over to the Yankee locker room to congratulate them. Managers didn't always do that. Me, I couldn't talk. I could not speak at all. I felt as if someone had died. It was the worst thing that ever happened. That cheap hit. Forty years later, I can still close my eyes and see it, still see Zeke diving for it and the ball squirting to the line. ..." It was the closest they would come to the pennant again in the Williams-DiMaggio-Doerr-Pesky years.

TED WILLIAMS, MICKEY HARRIS, DOMINIC DIMAGGIO,
PAUL CAMPBELL, JOHN PESKY, AND BOBBY DOERR,
LOUISVILLE SLUGGER BAT FACTORY, CIRCA 1947

NINE

TED WILLIAMS AND JOHN PESKY

It was over for them as teammates surprisingly soon. The last great season when they could compete at the highest level was 1950. That season Ted Williams smashed his elbow going after a fly ball during the All Star game, and he got only 334 at bats. The Korean War had started in June 1950 and

in May 1952 Williams was called back to duty as a Marine
Corps pilot. Though none of the four teammates realized it at
the time, that began the breakup of the group. Ted was 33 then,
and given the short career span of a great athlete, plus his service in World War Two, he probably, in any normal time, would
have been exempted from serving in Korea. But it was not a
normal time, and he was hardly alone in being called back. It
was not a popular war—it was not even called a war, but a
police action—and it did not capture the public imagination in
the way World War Two had. There was a desperate need for
men in all services, and there were a great many veterans of
World War Two in both the Army and the Marines, who, while
not actively serving in the reserves, discovered bitterly that they
had involuntarily left themselves open to recall. It was not a
happy time for them or for Ted Williams; Williams had considerable reason to think it was unjust, and to wonder if there
would be anything left of his career when he returned. Then he
might be, who knew—34 or 35 or even 36? He was smart
enough at that moment to keep his feelings to himself, aware
that if he protested with his unusually high visibility, he would
become the perfect target for all kinds of venom, from those
who were serving or who had relatives serving in Korea, and
from those who had never served, but who showed their uncommon patriotism through their typewriters. He was gone for
most of the 1952 and 1953 seasons, coming to bat only 10
times in 1952 and 91 times in 1953. By the time he returned,
his three close friends were no longer there. Bobby Doerr was

the first to go; the 1951 season was his last. Boston was playing in Cleveland on a cold night that year—the temperature was in the 40s, he remembered—and he came in to make the play on a slow ground ball. Suddenly he felt something go in his back, and he knew instantly that it was a serious injury. Soon he began to wear a corset every day to protect it. One morning he could no longer bend over to tie his shoes. He went to the ball-park and spent much of the day in the whirlpool, but it didn't seem to help. He took some time off and then came back for a game against the Philadelphia Athletics. "My first time up I took a swing, and I felt like someone had stabbed me, and I screamed out in pain," he remembered. Doerr went to the Leahy Clinic, where the doctors told him that a disc in his spine had worn out, and the vertebrae were rubbing against each other.

Charlie Keller, the Yankees' powerfully built outfielder, Doerr knew, had struggled with much the same thing at the end of his career. An operation might help or it might not, the doctors said—there was no way of telling. Doerr asked what would happen if he did not have the surgery and stopped playing in order not to further aggravate his back. Well, you'll probably have a normal life in two or three years, the lead orthopedist said. Doerr thought about it a long time. He loved playing baseball, but he was 33 at this point, and he had been doing it professionally since he was 16. His need to play the game was not as great anymore. What made it difficult was the knowledge that he had been at the top of the game just before the back injury; he knew the American League pitchers as he had not known them when he was younger, and in the preceding five years he had averaged well over 100 RBIs a season. But it was time to go. He and Monica talked about it, and they made the safe decision. Years later, he was still not sure why his back had given out so readily. He wondered if it had come from playing so much when he was so young; perhaps he had put too much pressure on his body when he was still growing. But there was nothing to do about that now. He walked away from his career after the 1951 season, and he did it without regrets.

John Pesky and Dom DiMaggio were soon gone too. Clearly the personnel was changing and changing quickly. Joe Cronin had been let go as manager after the 1947 season and had been bumped up to general manager; he was replaced, to almost everyone's surprise, by Joe McCarthy, the longtime Yankee manager. McCarthy was not an especially good fit in Boston; his bouts with alcohol, long a problem, became more frequent and more serious. He clearly believed that Tom Yawkey had run something of a country club operation and that it was his job to substitute if not exactly tough love—a phrase that had not yet been minted—then at least a colder eye and an iron hand for the lenient ways of Cronin. McCarthy lasted into the middle of the 1950 season, when he was replaced by Steve O'Neill, who had formerly managed Cleveland and Detroit. O'Neill was not around very long either. In 1951 the Red Sox traded for Lou Boudreau, the boy wonder of the Cleveland Indians, who had become the Indians' player-manager at age 24; to the Boston players, it was obvious that he was a manager-in-waiting, and in 1952 he took over the team. This did not bode well for either Pesky or DiMaggio. Boudreau was not eager to have veteran players roughly his own age on the team, especially ones with deeper roots in the organization. To this day, passionate Red Sox fans of that era remain embittered about Boudreau for getting rid of their personal heroes before their time was up, and for bringing players up from the minors before they were ready: "Lou Boudreau," said Dick Flavin, "did more damage to the Red Sox as their manager than he ever did playing against us in an Indians uniform."

Dominic DiMaggio was immediately suspicious of Boudreau, sensing that he wanted to bring up his own people. He sensed his own time was limited now and warned Pesky to be careful. He turned out to be right. After playing only 25 games for Boston in 1952, Pesky was traded to Detroit. He played the equivalent of two seasons with the Tigers, and in 1954 was traded to the Washington Senators, finishing his career there that year. He had hated being traded from the Red Sox. "I loved it in Boston. I wanted to play here forever, but I also knew the game, and that it was a business, and that you could not control things. And I knew most of our group was gone. Ted was in Korea, Bobby had retired, and Dominic knew he was going to be gone. So it was over, and I knew it."

Dom understood that he was going to be next. He had an infection in his left eye during the winter of 1952–53, and he almost missed spring training in 1953. His doctor had told him not to go, but if he did to be careful and not put any strain on the eye. Dominic believed that Boudreau tried to push him into the spring training lineup too soon. Then, on opening day, Boudreau started Tom Umphlett, a rookie, in centerfield, leaving Dominic on the bench with no explanation. Dominic was furious, and he asked for his release early in the season, after coming to bat only three times in three games. The previous year he had hit .294, just four points under his career average. He thought Boudreau's reading of talent was marginal: One of the players that Boudreau was particularly excited about was a young outfielder named Gene Stephens. "There was all this talk that he was going to be the next Ted Williams," Dominic said years later. "Boy, were they high on him. He was a good kid, but there was a terrible hitch in his swing, and I knew the pitchers would pick up on it very quickly. He couldn't pivot in his swing. I told Joe Cronin that he wouldn't hit .210. In fact I said I'd bet him $1,000 that he didn't hit .210. When they sent him down I think he was hitting .208." (Actually, Stephens hit .204 that season and became a career .240 hitter.)

It was a bad time in general for the Red Sox organization and its players and fans. The baseball world was going past them. Yawkey was still throwing money at young players, but the Red Sox organization, hardly alone in the big leagues in its narrowness—the Yankees were almost as bad—was blinded by race. Boston was going after young white players, and ignoring the great, new talent pool just opening up, that of young black ballplayers, most of whom in that generation went to the

National League. Boston had the first shot at Willie Mays because of its connection to the Birmingham Barons, a farm club of theirs. Mays played for the Birmingham Black Barons, who played in the white Barons' stadium, and Boston scout George Digby loved Mays. But despite Digby's rave reports, they inexplicably did not sign him. Well, there was an explanation, and it was race.

So it was that when Ted Williams returned from Korea, he came back to a different, younger, significantly less talented team. Not only were most of his old friends gone, but Willie Mays was not playing beside him in centerfield, able to run down balls for him and perhaps hitting either just in front of or right behind him in the batting order. Baseball was for him, always fun, but it was less fun after Korea when all his closest pals were gone.

JOHN PESKY, DOMINIC DIMAGGIO, BOBBY DOERR, MANAGER STEVE O'NEILL,
AND TED WILLIAMS AFTER DOERR ANNOUNCED HIS RETIREMENT
FROM BASEBALL, FENWAY PARK, 1951

TEN

BOBBY DOERR, JOHN PESKY, AND TED WILLIAMS AS
SPRING TRAINING INSTRUCTORS IN 1963

Growing old in America, the country of the young, is never easy, not even for those who have been successful in their lives and can afford the best medical care. Many of us, through the miracles of modern medicine,

outlive our parents by a significant span (although I am suscep-
tible to the same cardiovascular disease that my father had, I am
now 15 years older than he was when he died), but that makes
us vulnerable to a number of diseases that might have otherwise
never had a chance to manifest themselves.

When Dominic DiMaggio was about 45 years old he
began to have problems with his left hip. At first he assumed it
was just arthritis, but when it persisted and the pain became
acute, and his body began to change in other frightening ways,
he began to consult a variety of doctors. In time he was diagnosed with Paget's disease and referred to Dr. Stephen Krane at
Harvard Medical School. Krane is a distinguished rheumatolo-
gist and bone specialist, who is an expert on Paget's disease. Explaining just what causes Paget's is complicated—scientists are
still studying the causes, some of which are clearly genetic and
some of which may be environmental. The current theory is
that there is a genetic vulnerability, and a virus may strike when
the patient is young, perhaps in his or her teens, but lie dormant
for some 40 or 50 years. Then, much later in life, the body starts
producing bone material, overactively in fact—much as if the
patient were still a teenager—but which at this delayed point of
physical maturity profoundly and aberrantly affects the archi-
tecture of the body. "It is," says Charlene Waldman, the execu-
tive director of the Paget Foundation, "as if someone is building
a brick wall, and suddenly the pile of bricks is no longer even,
and the bricks are not lined up properly, and more bricks keep
being added." It can cause serious deformities, such as bowed

legs, bent spine and shoulders, enlarged skull, and the losses of hearing and several inches of height.

Dominic had a relatively severe case of Paget's, and his bowed legs and bent spine caused him to tilt forward. In time he lost a bit of height, something, he noted when he testified before a congressional committee about the disease, that he could ill afford. For an uncommonly proud man who had become a professional athlete against great odds, the disease was not merely an assault on his daily comfort but on his dignity as a man as well. Paget's, Dom later decided, was something that ran in his family; his father had probably suffered from it, though no one had realized it at the time, and perhaps his brothers Tom and Joe as well, though their cases had not been so serious.

For a long time there was relatively little in the way of treatment for the disease, but by the 1960s that began to change. When Dominic was first diagnosed, the principal medication was something called calcitonin, which was still experimental and had to be taken by injection three times a week. The idea of getting three shots a week for the rest of his life was not something Dominic was enthusiastic about. But Dr. Krane told him about a new, experimental treatment being used with some success in the Netherlands under the supervision of an immensely talented doctor named Olav Bijvoet. It was a medication called pamidronate, and although the results were very promising, it would be many years before the drug was approved for use in the United States. Among other things to recommend it was the fact that it could then be taken orally, rather than through injections. There was, it appeared, a very good chance that the treatment could arrest the deterioration of Dominic's body and greatly ease the pain. So Dominic and Emily flew to Holland to consult with Dr. Bijvoet. There Dominic started an intensive ten-day treatment program. One of the signs that a patient has some form of Paget's is an increase of an enzyme called serum alkaline phosphatase (SAP) in his blood. When the doctors checked Dominic's blood, he had an SAP count of 4,400, which was extremely high. During the ten-day intensive treatment, high doses of the medicine were injected into his arm, and he was put on a very strict diet. He was allowed two beers a day, though.

Six days into the treatment, he and Emily were in the hospital room when the doctors and the nurses filed in. Their faces all seemed glum. We don't have good news, Dr. Bijvoet said. What was wrong? Dominic asked. "We can't get your SAP count down now. So you'll have to take a six-month supply of tablets with you." That did not seem like such terrible news to Dominic, and he took his tablets faithfully as directed. Soon his count dropped to 1,600, and it has since fallen to 275.

The disease was arrested, and the pain considerably lessened. It will never go away entirely because so much damage had been done already. But, in terms of the previous treatments, the new one seemed nothing less than miraculous. The pain is still there sometimes in his hips and shoulders, and standing for a long period of time is difficult. At first he was reticent about stepping forward and calling attention to the disease, but as he became aware of the damage it was doing to those less fortunate than he and his admiration for his doctors grew, he became one of the principal spokesmen for those fighting the disease, sitting on the Paget Foundation board and lobbying as publicly as he could for resources to fight the disease.

B obby and Monica Doerr had been married for nine years when the first signs of her illness appeared. It was 1947, after the baseball season was over, and their son Donald was five years old. They were back in Illahe, walking across their property, when, about 400 yards from their home, she was hit by a sudden dizzy spell and started to weave in her tracks as if she were drunk. It was terrifying to both of them—here they were a young family with a young son and they wanted nothing more out of life than what they already had, and overnight this strong, radiant, fearless young woman seemed to have been struck down by a strange, inexplicable illness. That initiated a search for a doctor who could figure out what was happening, first locally, without much success, then in Eugene, a university town, and then finally, on the recommendation of doctors there, in Portland. There she was told that she more than likely had multiple sclerosis. The doctors prescribed B-12 vitamin shots for her and for a time the disease went into remission and she seemed to get better.

For 20 years, in fact, the disease disappeared, and they felt themselves uncommonly lucky. Then in 1967, when Bobby was coaching for Boston and the Red Sox made their miracle run for the pennant, she suddenly fell down in the street in Boston in the middle of the day. It happened out of the blue, with no warning, Bobby remembered, and she cracked a bone in a foot during the fall. Terrified, they consulted the doctors, who soon confirmed that the disease had returned, more virulently than ever. There was no remission now.

By 1972 Monica was using a cane, and by 1977 she had to use a walker; by the early '80s she was confined to a wheelchair. They were determined not to let the shadow of her illness change their lives or weaken their marriage. Bobby had always thought himself the luckiest man in the world—from the moment he saw her that day with her wonderful, red hair flowing out, and she had turned out to be the person he had envisioned. He knew that most people were not that lucky, that they saw something in someone across a room, and as often as not got it wrong, but in some miraculous way he and Moni had gotten it just right. Very few men spoke of their wives with as much respect and admiration as Bob Doerr spoke of Moni. They had never needed anyone else in their lives, and they were always grateful that they had been as lucky as they were. They were not about to let that change now.

She would not become an invalid, they vowed. They would make adjustments, not pull back from life, and they would try to do things just as if the illness had not struck. They would see their friends and travel when they wanted to. Their friends thought there was something unusually loving, even heroic, about the way they both dealt with this adversity. Yes, it was the way a great many other people thought they would deal with so potentially devastating an illness, but in reality, very few did. On reflection, no one who knew the Doerrs thought they would do otherwise. When Bobby made his annual trips to the Hall of Fame they either drove across the country in a specially rigged Suburban, with her wheelchair in the back, or flew together, with their travel plans carefully constructed for her maximum comfort. But there was no doubt that for all the courage and discipline they brought to dealing with her illness, there was a constant undertow of physical erosion. His own health was exceptionally good. In the fall of 2002 he was 84 years old, still strong and vigorous, still able to fish and enjoy the outdoors. The only sign that he had aged at all was a very slight stoop to his back, a reminder of the back problems that had driven him out of the game a half century earlier.

In 1999 Monica Doerr suffered the first of two strokes. Somewhat typically, Bobby blamed himself for what had happened. He had taken a prescribed medication, which had a terrible effect on him; he became dizzy for several days, losing his natural balance. He believed that his sudden vulnerability had a catastrophic effect on Monica. She became terribly nervous and anxious—he had never seen her like that before—and she did not easily come down from this high pitch of anxiety. He was convinced later that her fear had triggered the first of her two strokes, and he blamed himself for staying on the pills too long, and not alerting his doctor sooner about the problems he was having.

After the first stroke, she went into physical therapy and seemed for a time to make progress. Then, not long after, she suffered a second stroke. That affected her speech in a way that was immensely frustrating for her—she could understand everything being said in conversations, but she could not easily join in.

Ted Williams more than the others enjoyed exceptional health for a long time. There was nonetheless no small amount of disappointment in his private life, in terms of his failed marriages, and in his relationships with his three children—Bobby-Jo, from his first marriage, and John Henry and Claudia, from his third. Those relationships were often volatile; he knew he had not done well, and on occasion would talk in an oblique way of how he should have done better. Late in his life he developed a somewhat closer relationship with his one son, John Henry, but many of his friends thought it came at a high price for both of them. John Henry worked for Ted as his representative in personal appearances and the sale of Ted Williams memorabilia. This was not necessarily the healthiest thing—a young man who had had a difficult time finding his own way, and who was the son of a singularly famous and iconic father, making a living directly off his father's fame. (In June 2002, in what was one of the many unlikely episodes of this father-son saga, the Red Sox gave 33-year-old John Henry Williams a tryout with their team in the Florida rookie league. He went 0–3 in his first game, and the tryout did not last very long.)

The world of baseball appearances and memorabilia is not a particularly genteel one, but even so a number of serious people in that world deeply disliked dealing with John Henry Williams, and in time some of Ted's oldest friends felt they were being kept away from Ted because they had been critical of what they felt was John Henry's growing exploitation of his father. John Henry eventually left a string of bankruptcies in his wake, even though Ted's fame had always translated into something of a cash cow. John Henry was, the *Boston Globe*'s columnist Will McDonough wrote rather gently, a young man "who has a history of being involved in court-related matters." McDonough noted that John Henry was not particularly welcome in Fenway Park, where Red Sox officials wanted no part of him unless he was accompanied by Ted.

Late in Ted's life, his health beginning to break down ever

more quickly, some of his friends were shocked as the great hitter, his health obviously in terrible decline—he was 79 in 1998, and in a wheelchair and his eyesight was failing badly—was brought into memorabilia shows by his son to sign balls at $225 an autograph. On one occasion the session had to be stopped because Ted was so tired. His old friends felt that Ted seemed increasingly passive about the appearance business, and the driving force was obviously John Henry. More, almost everything appeared to be for sale, including the American flag that had hung in front of Ted's Hernando house, which in time came down and was soon autographed by the father and sold by the son on eBay. It was not surprising, many old friends thought, that after Ted died there was a bizarre family struggle between John Henry and Claudia and their half-sister Bobby-Jo, with the younger two children insisting that their father wished for his body to be frozen in a cryonic suspension tank. Some alleged that John Henry hoped to preserve samples of his father's DNA to sell for the benefit of would-be gifted hitters.

If there was considerable evidence that Ted had been flawed as both a husband and a parent, then nonetheless, there was immense respect—indeed reverence—elsewhere for him as a man, and as a figure in baseball history who seemed larger than life. The years when he felt he had to fight so much of the world around him were gone. Two things had happened—he had mellowed and the world had largely come round to him. Once he had feuded with a great many reporters. Now he got on exceptionally well with a younger generation of writers

who had been spared the ordeal of covering him as beat reporters when he was at his most tempestuous and the Boston
newspaper wars at their most vicious. Instead they had the good
fortune to come upon him in a new and more gentle incarnation when what distinguished him was the purity of his love of
the game and his almost unique generosity to younger players.

Then in the 1990s his body began to betray him, and he
suffered two strokes. He was confined to a wheelchair and able
to do less and less for himself, and his spirits were terrible. In
December 2000 the question facing the medical experts who
dealt with him was whether or not to go ahead to try to repair
a leaky heart valve. The issue was whether it was advisable to
perform such radical surgery on someone so old (and whether
such treatment would not be of greater benefit to someone
younger, given the medical energies and expense it required).
By then his health was desperate—he could no longer sleep
and was quite confused much of the time, becoming frailer by
the day. In mid-January 2001, attended by 14 doctors, nurses,
and technicians, Ted Williams, then 82, underwent almost ten
hours of open-heart surgery. His health did improve for a time,
and there was a feeling that the operation bought him one
more year of life, though the quality of life in that final year was
terrible.

In those last months it was Dominic who saw him most
often and in whom he confided. Life had become more and
more painful, the depression that came with declining capabil-
ities ever deeper. Dom tried to sympathize by talking about the

decline in his own health, dealing with Paget's, and about the quadruple bypass he had undergone in the fall of 2000. He talked also about what it had been like dealing with his brother in Joe's final weeks. But it was hard. There were two occasions in Ted's final months when he turned to Dominic and asked plaintively, "Dommy, Why? Why? Why?" Dominic knew he meant, Why am I so sick? Why is this happening to me? And of course, what's next for me?

Dominic would try, as best he could, to explain these things that could never be explained. "Teddy, we're all dealt a hand, and we don't really understand the hand we've been given. None of us do, but we do the best we can, for all of our lives. The whole world is proud of the way you played the hand you were given and of what you've done with your life." The first time the subject had come up, Dominic believed, it had been hard for Ted to accept his words, to understand how it had all come down to this, to feeling so weak and vulnerable as a man, but then afterwards when he slipped a bit more and became unusually depressed and Dominic would talk to him in the same vein, he seemed to understand it better. Dominic thought it was extremely painful to watch a man who had always been so physical and so powerful and whose pleasures had come from the use of his body and his uncommon physical attributes—and who had been so *independent* because of those special gifts—now wither away and feel so frail and vulnerable, and so dependent on others.

In the last few weeks that Dom had talked to him over the phone in August and September 2001, just before the three men made their final pilgrimage, the slippage was obvious. Dom would call every day by phone, and they would talk, mostly about what the Red Sox were doing, and sometimes Ted would nod off in the middle of a sentence, lose his thought, and there would be silence at the other end of the phone. Sometimes Dom would say, "Teddy, are you there?" Sometimes there would be the answer, "Yes, I'm here, Dommy, I'm here," and sometimes there would be no answer at all.

BOBBY AND MONICA DOERR,
FIFTIETH WEDDING ANNIVERSARY,
OCTOBER 24, 1988

ELEVEN

DOMINIC DiMAGGIO, TED WILLIAMS, AND JOHN PESKY,
OCTOBER 2001

T he voyage of Dominic, John, and Dick Flavin from
Marion to Hernando took three full days. All three
men in the car were proud that they never turned the
radio on, not once. Dominic loved the opera and had brought
along a few tapes, and on occasion they played one, mostly

Pavarotti and Domingo. But never the radio. There was just too much to say, too much to reminisce about, and they knew they would never be together again like this. This was the last time. Much of the talk was about Ted. They laughed about him playing in the outfield; he was not exactly the most graceful left-fielder of our time, although sometimes they had claimed to reporters that he was. The truth was that his body parts never quite seemed to fit; it was as if his long legs had been joined at the last minute to an upper body which was fabricated somewhere else, and the two halves were never really reconciled to each other. It was not that he ran that badly, but he always looked like he ran badly; nothing was quite in synch the way it was with Joe DiMaggio, who seemed to do everything so effortlessly. Ted himself even laughed about his war cry from left field when a ball was hit in his general direction: "You take it, Dommy! You take it!" Ted had even mentioned it in a letter he wrote late in his life pushing Dominic for the Hall of Fame. They had teased him back then that Dom should have gotten part of his salary because he did so much of Ted's work in the outfield.

The three men spent a night in Roanoke, Virginia, and then the next day drove the roughly 700 miles to Hernando, in Central Florida. They did not try to see Ted that night, but waited until the following morning, when they drove over to his house. It had all come down to this one, final visit. They had once felt immortal, so sure of their youth and their strength and their futures, so immune to the vagaries of age. They had made it through the Depression and World War Two. True, they had never overtaken the Yankees the way they had hoped, and in the Cardinal Series, Harry Brecheen had done them in. Who would ever have thought it would be Harry Brecheen? But in three games and 20 innings his earned run average had been 0.45, and it had not been a fluke; he had three more good seasons after that.

Hernando was a relatively new place for Ted, and for the three of them. For years he had loved living in Islamorada in the Keys, in one of the great fishing spots in the country. Moving inland to Hernando was probably an early sign that he was getting a little old. But Islamorada had become overdeveloped and a lot less fun for serious fishermen, and a number of the old-time guides who were his friends had passed away. Ted had a friend who was a real estate developer, who offered him a home in one of his developments, plus a small percentage of homes sold in the development. In return he got to use Ted in his promotions. The house had a big number nine on the gate—Ted's old number—and the code to open the gate was equally fitting: Star 1941.

Of the three of them, Dominic was the best prepared for what they were about to see because he had visited Ted in San Diego where he was rehabilitating after his heart surgery. The other two did not know what to expect, and when the attendants wheeled Ted in, they gasped in shock. Here was their old friend, a man once supremely powerful, shrunken now, down to perhaps 130 pounds, head down on his chest. John looked as if he were having a heart attack—and, he later said, he thought he might actually have one, right there and then. He was trying to hold back the tears, and Flavin was just as numb, wondering if he should be there at all, if somehow he wasn't intruding on something terribly private. But there was Dominic, racing across the room, and yelling, "Teddy, Teddy! It's Dommy, Teddy, it's Dommy! And John is here too! And Dick Flavin!"

Then slowly Ted's head came up, and he started to grin. They began to talk, and Ted had asked Dom how the Queen was, a reference to the much-loved Emily. Soon Dominic brought up one of Ted's most joyous moments, the time back in 1941 when they still played the All Star Game to win. It was such a serious game back then that in the ninth inning, with the National League leading 5–3, Ted and Joe DiMaggio were still in the game. The bases were loaded with one out and Joe, who was batting ahead of Ted, hit what should have been a double-play ball, but second baseman Billy Herman's throw to first was wide, making it 5–4, with two outs. Then, with Claude Passeau of the Cubs on the mound, Ted hit a ball into the upper deck of Tiger Stadium to give the American League a 7–5 victory. And he, usually so careful in registering pleasure, mostly because of his relationship with the Boston media and fans—his motto seemed to be "Keep it private," there was no need to share the pleasure of the deeds—had gone around the bases like a young colt, clapping his hands together, exuberant and joyous, the pleasure so obvious, to be shared this time with everyone.

Now, in his wheelchair, Ted was suddenly in charge again.

It was fascinating to watch him become stronger by the minute with the arrival of his friends. He had to take charge, of course, because that was the natural order of things and that was what his friends wanted. Hovering in the background, the nurses played some old Sinatra songs on the CD player, and Ted was saying that he was a hell of a singer, this guy, and Flavin mentioned a benefit a few years ago when Sinatra had showed up expressly for the purpose of meeting Ted Williams. Ted said he remembered meeting him. Then he added that Sinatra was special, in his words, "a big feeling guy," which translated into a guy with a big ego. "But hell," he added, "he had a right to be a big feeling guy—he was a hell of a singer."

There were from time to time different signs of his decline. At one point they went into the kitchen, where there were small porcelain mementoes of Ted's late dog, Slugger, a Dalmatian. Slugger had been a gift from Lou, who herself had died several years ago. That Ted had ended up with a dog surprised everyone at the time, and no one expected a warm relationship, given the level of impatience and perfection for which Ted was noted. Could a dog ever really come up to his standards? But his friends were in for a surprise: Ted grew to love the dog, and now in the kitchen he was saying what a hell of a dog Slugger had been. Then someone asked what breed of dog he was, and Ted said he was a German shepherd.

Then there were the quizzes. Ted was dominating the three of them now, and he started doing quizzes with them. "I'm thinking of a guy, a Yankee," Ted said. "Initials: P.T. A hell of a clutch hitter. Can you name him?" Well, they all tried that one, but no one could get it, they all struck out. Finally Ted gave them the answer, which was Paul O'Neill, who was an under-rated ballplayer for a long time and whom Ted had admired because he had maximized his at bats and played the game hard. P.O.? P.T.? Hell, it was obvious that Ted had been right. Then he said he was thinking of who was the single most underrated ballplayer of their era. There was a lot of guessing, and someone suggested Roy Sievers, a very tough power hitter whose mis-fortune it was to play with the St. Louis Browns and then with the Washington Senators for much of his career. Someone else suggested another player, Roy Cullenbine, again a tough hitter, much-traveled (6 clubs in 10 years), also wrong. Only Ted knew the answer, which was Eddie Robinson, another formidable hitter, a man with genuine power, but also well-traveled, 8 teams in 13 years. So he was right again.

Then Ted talked about Ted Lyons of the White Sox, a ter-rific pitcher; Ted admired him because he was so smart, and Ted did not go around saying that of many pitchers. But Lyons had always kept him off balance; when Ted guessed breaking ball, it would be the heater, and when he guessed fastball, it would be the breaking ball. Goddamn smart, that Ted Lyons.

There was a lot of talk about Bobby Doerr, and how they had to police themselves when they were young because Bobby didn't swear. Also about how good he was, with that smooth footwork and the great glove hand. There was a little bit of a hole in the visit, Flavin thought, because Bobby was not there. "But if Bobby was here," John said, "we couldn't say all the things we're saying now."

They visited with Ted for two days, two visits a day, each one not too long, because he needed his naps. On the last visit, Dominic suddenly said, "Teddy, I'm going to sing you a song." It was an Italian love song, the story of two men who were best friends, one of whom was in love with a girl. But he was afraid to tell her, so he did it through his friend, who then stole her away. "I Love Her, But I Don't Know How to Tell Her," Dominic called it. Then Dominic began to sing and the house was filled with the sound of his beautiful baritone voice. Ted loved it, he started clapping, and so Dominic sang it again, and Ted clapped again. Then Dominic sang "Me and My Shadow" for him. "Dommy, Dommy, you did really well," Ted said when he finished. Then finally Flavin, not to be outdone, and being Irish, sang, "I'll Take You Home Again, Kathleen." He, too, sang well, it was decided, although not, in Dominic's judgment, as well as Dominic himself. Then it was time to go, Dominic to his home near Palm Beach and John and Dick back to Boston by plane.

Before he left, Dominic asked Ted whether or not he was getting the baseball scores, and apparently he was not; no one, he said, told him anything anymore. When the next season started, Dominic called him every morning with the latest Red Sox score and an update on how they were playing. If Dominic called a little late, Ted's attendants would tell him that Ted had been asking about him and whether he had called in yet. Then in the final weeks, Ted became weaker and weaker, and it was hard for Dominic to tell whether he was still there at the end of the line, because sometimes he would slip out of consciousness in the middle of a call. There had been one final call when Dominic had called in and sensed a silence at the other end and he had asked, "Teddy are you there," and Josh, Ted's attendant, had said, "No, he's fallen asleep." "Well, please tell him I called," Dominic said, and the next day Ted died.

A few months after Ted died, I found myself in Johnny Pesky's house in Swampscott, starting work on this book. When I had first called his home to set up the meeting, Ruth Pesky told me that he was already at the ballpark working. "He's eighty-two," she said. "He promised me he'd quit when he got to eighty, but he didn't. But I do think he'll quit when he reaches eighty-five."

It's a lovely home. A painting by Leroy Neiman of Ted Williams and that marvelous swing hangs in the living room, and the air is scented by Pesky's ever-present cigars. He and Ruth Hickey Pesky have lived in this house for 35 years, and they built it to their specifications. It's a bit modern, with a good deal of light coming in, and it has a warm feeling of being lived in. It took 22 years to pay off the mortgage, which amuses Pesky because he coaches now in an age when young ballplayers can pay off their mortgages in one year, thanks to their awesome salaries.

Some of the difference in attitude is, I suppose, generational. Pesky, like the other three, grew up in an America of dramatically lower expectations and came of age during the Depression. A great deal less was assumed in terms of lifestyle. But no small part of it was the nature of the man himself. He had always understood his limitations and his strengths, both on and off the field, and thus the sum of his good fortune. Besides, if his head had swelled even slightly, Ruth Pesky was always there to bring him back down. His fame, he enjoyed pointing out, mattered not at all to her.

Pesky was in no way disappointed with what had *not* taken place during the rest of his life. Instead he seemed somewhat in awe of how long it had all lasted, how rich his life had been, how many friends he had made, how many people actually liked him, and how many people still remembered him and his glory days, and were pleased to be in his company. It was never about money, he said. The money was okay, less surely than it should have been because of labor laws of the time. Still it was more than anything he might have made doing another job— no one was beating a rush to their door to offer someone named John Paveskovich a job. Johnny Pesky was another matter. Perhaps the alternative might have been working for the sawmill like his father.

But baseball had provided a wonderful, rich life. The pleasure had always been in the doing, the sheer delight in going out there every day and playing, being paid to do the thing you loved to do. And the richness had come from the friendships, he said. How many people in other professions have friendships that last so long—unusual friendships because when you see each other, you were instantly taken back to another time, when you were all young, and some big game was on the line.

If there was one thing that surprised Pesky, it was how long it had all lasted—how much resonance there was to his fame, even now, 60 years after he broke in. People still knew who he was and still cared about him and his teammates. There was a special richness, he thought, to the kind of life he had lived that went well beyond any material rewards.

The other three, I thought, all agreed. "My guys," Ted had called them, and they were that, always very much their own men, but his guys as well, forever linked to him as well as to each other. When Bobby Doerr and Dominic DiMaggio talked about their lives, it was with the same tone as John, with an appreciation—indeed a gratitude—for their good fortune, and a sense that although they had prospered, the best part, the richest part, of their lives had little to do with material things, and that they had lived their lives with very few regrets.

AUTHOR'S NOTE

In January 2002, I went to Palm Beach to lecture to a community group, and I flew in a day early in order to have dinner with Dominic and Emily DiMaggio. The three of us spent a lovely evening together and in the course of it Dominic told me the story of his last trip, along with John Pesky and Dick Flavin, to see Ted Williams. It struck me almost immediately that it might make a small book, and that the kind of intense friendship the four teammates enjoyed was unusual, not just in sports, but in general in a society like ours. Writing the book, I received nothing but uncommon cooperation from the three surviving Boston players, Dominic, Bobby Doerr, and John Pesky, all of whom I had kept in touch with since meeting them while doing *Summer of '49*. I would like to thank all three of them for their cooperation, and I would also like to thank Emily DiMaggio for her generosity and for the remarkable quality of her friendship over the years. She is, in terms of friendship, a true gamer, and she lets no one fall to the wayside.

It struck me while I was doing the book how lucky I was. An old friend of mine, the writer Russell Baker, hearing what I was doing told me, "That's not work—that's stealing." Rarely is work so pleasurable; in this case, mostly, I think it was due to the natures of the four men who are at the center of the book.

Let me thank in addition Dick Flavin, both for his help on this book and for the slice of the old Green Monster he sent me 14 years ago, Monica and Donald Doerr, Ruth Pesky, Dan Shaughnessy (the talented *Boston Globe* baseball writer and columnist who is exceptionally generous to straphangers like me), Dick Bresciani of the Red Sox, Boo Ferriss, Mel Parnell, Bob Broeg, Paul DiMaggio, Emily DiMaggio (Emily the younger, that is, Dominic and Emily's daughter), Marty Nolan, Curtis Willkie, Glen Stout, Tom Wicker, Linda Drogin, my pal David Fine, of Nantucket, who once lived near Dominic back in the early '40s, when Dominic was single, and my late uncle, Harry Levy, who had season tickets to Fenway and who took me to Fenway Park in 1946. Let me also thank Dave Chase of the National Pastime in Memphis, a museum of minor league baseball, and the staff of the A. Bartlett Giamatti Research Center at the National Baseball Hall of Fame in Cooperstown, New York, for assistance far and beyond the call of duty.

I am indebted as ever to my own support team, my lawyer-agents, Marty Garbus and Bob Solomon, and Fredda Tourin; the wondrous Phillip Roome who takes my convoluted travel schedule and makes sense out of it; Carolyn Parqueth who types my notes under considerable deadline pressure; Bob Miller, Will Schwalbe, Ellen Archer, Jane Comins, Michael Burkin, Beth Dickey, and Kiera Hepford of Hyperion; Lesley Krauss; as well as Doug Stumpf and Stephen Levey, who edited the book.

APPENDIX: STATISTICS

Key to Abbreviations

AG:	age that year
TM:	team
G:	games played
AB:	at bats
H:	hits
2B:	doubles
3B:	triples
HR:	home runs
R:	runs scored
RBI:	runs batted in
SB:	stolen bases
BB:	base on balls
SO:	strikeouts
BA:	batting average
OBP:	on base percentage
SLG:	slugging percentage
FP:	fielding percentage
BOLD:	league leader

DOM DIMAGGIO

Dominic Paul DiMaggio

Year	Ag	Tm	G	AB	H	2B	3B	HR
1940	23	BOS	108	418	126	32	6	8
1941	24	BOS	144	584	165	37	6	8
1942	25	BOS	151	622	178	36	8	14
1946	29	BOS	142	534	169	24	7	7
1947	30	BOS	136	513	145	21	5	8
1948	31	BOS	155	**648**	185	40	4	9
1949	32	BOS	145	605	186	34	5	8
1950	33	BOS	141	588	193	30	**11**	7
1951	34	BOS	146	**639**	189	34	4	12
1952	35	BOS	128	486	143	20	1	6
1953	36	BOS	3	3	1	0	0	0
11 Seasons			1399	5640	1680	308	57	87

1946 World Series	G	AB	H	2B	3B	HR
	7	27	7	3	0	0

Bats Right, *Throws* Right   *Debut* April 16, 1940
Height 5'9", *Weight* 168 lb.   *Born* February 12, 1917, in
                                    San Francisco, CA

R	RBI	SB	BB	SO	BA	OBP	SLG	FP
81	46	7	41	46	.301	.367	.464	.977
117	58	13	90	57	.283	.385	.408	.964
110	48	16	70	52	.286	.364	.437	.987
85	73	10	66	58	.316	.393	.427	.985
75	71	10	74	62	.283	.376	.390	.977
127	87	10	101	58	.285	.383	.401	.981
126	60	9	96	55	.307	.404	.420	.977
131	70	**15**	82	68	.328	.414	.452	.983
113	72	4	73	53	.296	.370	.418	.973
81	33	6	57	61	.294	.371	.377	.975
0	0	0	0	1	.333	.333	.333	—
1046	618	100	750	571	.298	.383	.419	.978

R	RBI	SB	BB	SO	BA	OBP	SLG
2	3	0	2	2	.259	.310	.370

Appendix

BOBBY DOERR

Robert Pershing Doerr

Year	Ag	Tm	G	AB	H	2B	3B	HR
1937	19	BOS	55	147	33	5	1	2
1938	20	BOS	145	509	147	26	7	5
1939	21	BOS	127	525	167	28	2	12
1940	22	BOS	151	595	173	37	10	22
1941	23	BOS	132	500	141	28	4	16
1942	24	BOS	144	545	158	35	5	15
1943	25	BOS	**155**	604	163	32	3	16
1944	26	BOS	125	468	152	30	10	15
1946	28	BOS	151	583	158	34	9	18
1947	29	BOS	146	561	145	23	10	17
1948	30	BOS	140	527	150	23	6	27
1949	31	BOS	139	541	167	30	9	18
1950	32	BOS	149	586	172	29	**11**	27
1951	33	BOS	106	402	116	21	2	13

14 Seasons			1865	7093	2042	381	89	223

1946 World Series	G	AB	H	2B	3B	HR
	6	22	9	1	0	1

Bats Right, *Throws* Right
Height 5'11", *Weight* 175 lb.

Debut April 20, 1937
Born April 7, 1918, in
Los Angeles, CA

R	RBI	SB	BB	SO	BA	OBP	SLG	FP
22	14	2	18	25	.224	.313	.313	.973
70	80	5	59	39	.289	.363	.397	.968
75	73	1	38	32	.318	.365	.448	.976
87	105	10	57	53	.291	.353	.497	.977
74	93	1	43	43	.282	.339	.450	.971
71	102	4	67	55	.290	.369	.455	.975
78	75	8	62	59	.270	.339	.412	.990
95	81	5	58	31	.325	.399	**.528**	.976
95	116	5	66	67	.271	.346	.453	.986
79	95	3	59	47	.258	.329	.426	.981
94	111	3	83	49	.285	.386	.505	.993
91	109	2	75	33	.309	.393	.497	.980
103	120	3	67	42	.294	.367	.519	.988
60	73	2	57	33	.289	.378	.448	.981
1094	1247	54	809	608	.288	.362	.461	.980

R	RBI	SB	BB	SO	BA	OBP	SLG
1	3	0	2	2	.409	.458	.591

JOHNNY PESKY

John Michael Pesky

Born John Michael Paveskovich

Year	Ag	Tm	G	AB	H	2B	3B	HR
1942	22	BOS	147	620	**205**	29	9	2
1946	26	BOS	153	**621**	**208**	43	4	2
1947	27	BOS	155	**638**	**207**	27	8	0
1948	28	BOS	143	565	159	26	6	3
1949	29	BOS	148	604	185	27	7	2
1950	30	BOS	127	490	153	22	6	1
1951	31	BOS	131	480	150	20	6	3
1952	32	BOS	25	67	10	2	0	0
		DET	69	177	45	4	0	1
		TOT	94	244	55	6	0	1
1953	33	DET	103	308	90	22	1	2
1954	34	DET	20	17	3	0	0	1
		WSH	49	158	40	4	3	0
		TOT	69	175	43	4	3	1
10 Seasons			1270	4745	1455	226	50	17

1946 World Series	G	AB	H	2B	3B	HR
	7	30	7	0	0	0

Bats Left, *Throws* Right

Height 5'9", *Weight* 168 lb.

Debut April 14, 1942

Born September 27, 1919, in
Portland, OR

R	RBI	SB	BB	SO	BA	OBP	SLG	FP
105	51	12	42	36	.331	.375	.416	.955
115	55	9	65	29	.335	.401	.427	.969
106	39	12	72	22	.324	.393	.392	.976
124	55	3	99	32	.281	.394	.365	.951
111	69	8	100	19	.306	.408	.384	.970
112	49	2	104	31	.312	.437	.388	.973
93	41	2	84	15	.312	.417	.398	.958
10	2	0	15	5	.149	.313	.179	.925
26	9	1	41	11	.254	.394	.294	.958
36	11	1	56	16	.225	.372	.262	.952
43	24	3	27	10	.292	.353	.390	.991
5	1	0	3	1	.176	.300	.353	—
17	9	1	10	7	.253	.296	.316	.979
22	10	1	13	8	.246	.296	.320	.979
867	404	53	662	218	.307	.394	.386	.966

R	RBI	SB	BB	SO	BA	OBP	SLG
2	0	1	1	3	.233	.258	.233

TED WILLIAMS

Theodore Samuel Williams

Year	Ag	Tm	G	AB	H	2B	3B	HR
1939	20	BOS	149	565	185	44	11	31
1940	21	BOS	144	561	193	43	14	23
1941	22	BOS	143	456	185	33	3	**37**
1942	23	BOS	150	522	186	34	5	**36**
1946	27	BOS	150	514	176	37	8	38
1947	28	BOS	156	528	181	40	9	**32**
1948	29	BOS	137	509	188	**44**	3	25
1949	30	BOS	**155**	566	194	**39**	3	**43**
1950	31	BOS	89	334	106	24	1	28
1951	32	BOS	148	531	169	28	4	30
1952	33	BOS	6	10	4	0	1	1
1953	34	BOS	37	91	37	6	0	13
1954	35	BOS	117	386	133	23	1	29
1955	36	BOS	98	320	114	21	3	28
1956	37	BOS	136	400	138	28	2	24
1957	38	BOS	132	420	163	28	1	38

APPENDIX

Bats Left, *Throws* Right
Height 6'3", *Weight* 205 lb.

Debut April 20, 1939
Born August 30, 1918, in
San Diego, CA
Died July 5, 2002, in
Inverness, FL

R	RBI	SB	BB	SO	BA	OBP	SLG	FP
131	**145**	2	107	64	.327	.436	.609	.945
134	113	4	96	54	.344	**.442**	.594	.960
135	120	2	**147**	27	**.406**	**.553**	**.735**	.961
141	**137**	3	**145**	51	**.356**	**.499**	**.648**	.988
142	123	0	**156**	44	.342	**.497**	**.667**	.971
125	**114**	0	**162**	47	**.343**	**.499**	**.634**	.975
124	127	4	**126**	41	**.369**	**.497**	**.615**	.983
150	**159**	1	**162**	48	.343	**.490**	**.650**	.983
82	97	3	82	21	.317	.452	.647	.956
109	126	1	**144**	45	.318	**.464**	**.556**	.988
2	3	0	2	2	.400	.500	.900	1.000
17	34	0	19	10	.407	.509	.901	.970
93	89	0	**136**	32	.345	.513	**.635**	.982
77	83	2	91	24	.356	.496	.703	.989
71	82	0	102	39	.345	**.479**	.605	.973
96	87	0	119	43	**.388**	**.526**	**.731**	.995

(continued)

(Ted Williams continued)

| | | | | | | | | *(continued)* |
Year	Ag	Tm	G	AB	H	2B	3B	HR
1958	39	BOS	129	411	135	23	2	26
1959	40	BOS	103	272	69	15	0	10
1960	41	BOS	113	310	98	15	0	29
19 Seasons			2292	7706	2654	525	71	521

1946 World Series			G	AB	H	2B	3B	HR
			7	25	5	0	0	0

(continued)

R	RBI	SB	BB	SO	BA	OBP	SLG	FP
81	85	1	98	49	**.328**	**.458**	.584	.957
32	43	0	52	27	.254	.372	.419	.970
56	72	1	75	41	.316	.451	.645	.993
1798	1839	24	2021	709	.344	**.482**	.634	.974

R	RBI	SB	BB	SO	BA	OBP	SLG	
2	1	0	5	5	.200	.333	.200	

BOSTON RED SOX TEAM STANDINGS

Key to Abbreviations	
W:	wins
L:	losses
WL%:	win/loss percentage
GB:	games behind

1937 American League

Team	W	L	WL%	GB
Yankees	102	52	.662	—
Tigers	89	65	.578	13.0
White Sox	86	68	.558	16.0
Indians	83	71	.539	19.0
Red Sox	**80**	**72**	**.526**	**21.0**
Senators	73	80	.477	28.5
Athletics	54	97	.358	46.5
Browns	46	108	.299	56.0

1938 American League

Team	W	L	WL%	GB
Yankees	99	53	.651	—
Red Sox	**88**	**61**	**.591**	**9.5**
Indians	86	66	.566	13.0
Tigers	84	70	.545	16.0
Senators	75	76	.497	23.5
White Sox	65	83	.439	32.0
Browns	55	97	.362	44.0
Athletics	53	99	.349	46.0

1939 American League

Team	W	L	WL%	GB
Yankees	106	45	.702	—
Red Sox	**89**	**62**	**.589**	**17.0**
Indians	87	67	.565	20.5
White Sox	85	69	.552	22.5
Tigers	81	73	.526	26.5
Senators	65	87	.428	41.5
Athletics	55	97	.362	51.5
Browns	43	111	.279	64.5

1940 American League

Team	W	L	WL%	GB
Tigers	90	64	.584	—
Indians	89	65	.578	1.0
Yankees	88	66	.571	2.0
Red Sox	**82**	**72**	**.532**	**8.0**
White Sox	82	72	.532	8.0
Browns	67	87	.435	23.0
Senators	64	90	.416	26.0
Athletics	54	100	.351	36.0

APPENDIX

1941 American League

Team	W	L	WL%	GB
Yankees	101	53	.656	—
Red Sox	**84**	**70**	**.545**	**17.0**
White Sox	77	77	.500	24.0
Indians	75	79	.487	26.0
Tigers	75	79	.487	26.0
Browns	70	84	.455	31.0
Senators	70	84	.455	31.0
Athletics	64	90	.416	37.0

1942 American League

Team	W	L	WL%	GB
Yankees	103	51	.669	—
Red Sox	**93**	**59**	**.612**	**9.0**
Browns	82	69	.543	19.5
Indians	75	79	.487	28.0
Tigers	73	81	.474	30.0
White Sox	66	82	.446	34.0
Senators	62	89	.411	39.5
Athletics	55	99	.357	48.0

1943 American League

Team	W	L	WL%	GB
Yankees	98	56	.636	—
Senators	84	69	.549	13.5
Indians	82	71	.536	15.5
White Sox	82	72	.532	16.0
Tigers	78	76	.506	20.0
Browns	72	80	.474	25.0
Red Sox	**68**	**84**	**.447**	**29.0**
Athletics	49	105	.318	49.0

1944 American League

Team	W	L	WL%	GB
Browns	89	65	.578	—
Tigers	88	66	.571	1.0
Yankees	83	71	.539	6.0
Red Sox	**77**	**77**	**.500**	**12.0**
Indians	72	82	.468	17.0
Athletics	72	82	.468	17.0
White Sox	71	83	.461	18.0
Senators	64	90	.416	25.0

1945 American League

Team	W	L	WL%	GB
Tigers	88	65	.575	—
Senators	87	67	.565	1.5
Browns	81	70	.536	6.0
Yankees	81	71	.533	6.5
Indians	73	72	.503	11.0
White Sox	71	78	.477	15.0
Red Sox	**71**	**83**	**.461**	**17.5**
Athletics	52	98	.347	34.5

1946 American League

Team	W	L	WL%	GB
Red Sox	**104**	**50**	**.675**	**—**
Tigers	92	62	.597	12.0
Yankees	87	67	.565	17.0
Senators	76	78	.494	28.0
White Sox	74	80	.481	30.0
Indians	68	86	.442	36.0
Browns	66	88	.429	38.0
Athletics	49	105	.318	55.0

1946 World Series

Game 1	**Red Sox** 3–Cardinals 2
Game 2	Red Sox 0–**Cardinals** 3
Game 3	Cardinals 0–**Red Sox** 4
Game 4	**Cardinals** 12–Red Sox 3
Game 5	Cardinals 3–**Red Sox** 6
Game 6	Red Sox 1–**Cardinals** 4
Game 7	Red Sox 3–**Cardinals** 4

1947 American League

Team	W	L	WL%	GB
Yankees	97	57	.630	—
Tigers	85	69	.552	12.0
Red Sox	**83**	**71**	**.539**	**14.0**
Indians	80	74	.519	17.0
Athletics	78	76	.506	19.0
White Sox	70	84	.455	27.0
Senators	64	90	.416	33.0
Browns	59	95	.383	38.0

Appendix

1948 American League				
Team	W	L	WL%	GB
Indians	97	58	.626	—
Red Sox	**96**	**59**	**.619**	**1.0**
Yankees	94	60	.610	2.5
Athletics	84	70	.545	12.5
Tigers	78	76	.506	18.5
Browns	59	94	.386	37.0
Senators	56	97	.366	40.0
White Sox	51	101	.336	44.5

1949 American League				
Team	W	L	WL%	GB
Yankees	97	57	.630	—
Red Sox	**96**	**58**	**.623**	**1.0**
Indians	89	65	.578	8.0
Tigers	87	67	.565	10.0
Athletics	81	73	.526	16.0
White Sox	63	91	.409	34.0
Browns	53	101	.344	44.0
Senators	50	104	.325	47.0

1950 American League				
Team	W	L	WL%	GB
Yankees	98	56	.636	—
Tigers	95	59	.617	3.0
Red Sox	**94**	**60**	**.610**	**4.0**
Indians	92	62	.597	6.0
Senators	67	87	.435	31.0
White Sox	60	94	.390	38.0
Browns	58	96	.377	40.0
Athletics	52	102	.338	46.0

1951 American League				
Team	W	L	WL%	GB
Yankees	98	56	.636	—
Indians	93	61	.604	5.0
Red Sox	**87**	**67**	**.565**	**11.0**
White Sox	81	73	.526	17.0
Tigers	73	81	.474	25.0
Athletics	70	84	.455	28.0
Senators	62	92	.403	36.0
Browns	52	102	.338	46.0

1952 American League				
Team	W	L	WL%	GB
Yankees	95	59	.617	—
Indians	93	61	.604	2.0
White Sox	81	73	.526	14.0
Athletics	79	75	.513	16.0
Senators	78	76	.506	17.0
Red Sox	**76**	**78**	**.494**	**19.0**
Browns	64	90	.416	31.0
Tigers	50	104	.325	45.0

1953 American League				
Team	W	L	WL%	GB
Yankees	99	52	.656	—
Indians	92	62	.597	8.5
White Sox	89	65	.578	11.5
Red Sox	**84**	**69**	**.549**	**16.0**
Senators	76	76	.500	23.5
Tigers	60	94	.390	45.5
Athletics	59	95	.383	41.5
Browns	54	100	.351	46.5

ABOUT THE AUTHOR

DAVID HALBERSTAM, winner of the Pulitzer Prize for his reporting from Vietnam at the age of 30, is one of America's best-known journalists and historians. His last thirteen books have all been national best-sellers, five of them about sports, which Halberstam uses as a mirror to reflect the larger society. Both *The Best and the Brightest*, the story of how and why America went to war in Vietnam, and *Summer of '49*, about the Yankee–Red Sox pennant race, went to number one on the *New York Times* best-seller list. Halberstam is a member of the elective Society of American Historians and is currently completing a book on the events of late November 1950, when massive numbers of Chinese soldiers struck at greatly outnumbered American forces along the Chongchon and Yalu rivers in North Korea.

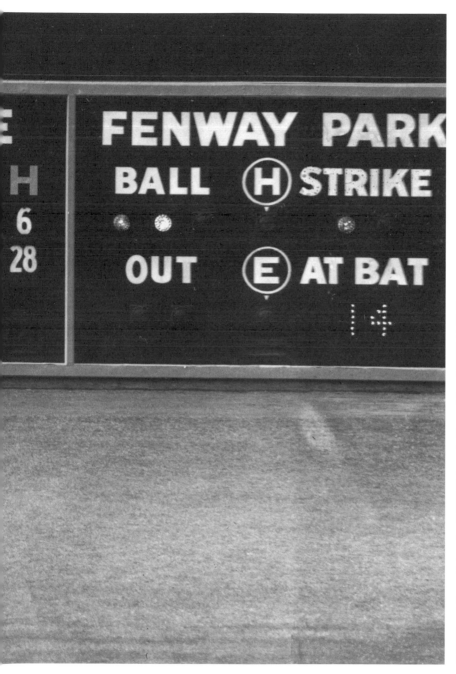

Ted Williams at Fenway Park on June 8, 1950. Photo used with permission of AP-Worldwide Photos.